ABSCAM Ethics:
Moral Issues and Deception in Law Enforcement

Edited by Gerald M. Caplan
The Police Foundation

Library of Congress Catalog Card Number: 82–74444

Contents

174
ab 88C

Preface

Although the use of informants and undercover agents has long been recognized as vital to successful law enforcement, only recently has that use become the subject of systematic public scrutiny. And nothing did more to heighten that scrutiny than the use of informants and undercover agents in the FBI's ABSCAM investigation of members of Congress. Given the element of deception in government use of informants and undercover agents, it is not surprising that serious civil liberties questions and major ethical issues have been raised about ABSCAM and similar operations. Clearly, expert opinion is deeply divided about both the necessity for ABSCAM-type investigations and the particulars of such operations.

Equally clear is the need to focus scholarly and professional attention on the ABSCAM thicket. As law enforcement officials, judges, and academics weigh the value and the limitations of undercover operations, something approaching a consensus will emerge about the best way to control and manage these operations. These operations must mesh with both democratic values and the need for public order and integrity in government. But for now, the most that can be said is this: All the contributors to this book agree that certain types of crimes can be detected only by using deception and employing informants. On all other matters, the differences are great.

This book has its origins in a conference on deceptive enforcement techniques held at Harvard University on April 16 and 17, 1981, and sponsored by the Hastings Institute of Society, Ethics, and the Life Sciences. The motivating force behind the conference was Sissela Bok to whom all persons interested in the subject of ethics in law enforcement are indebted. Five of this book's authors attended the conference, some presenting papers that are chapters, and two of the authors presented their materials at the conference on police ethics at the John Jay College of Criminal Justice of the City University of New York on April 24, 1982. These conferences were important in bringing to the forum of public debate the issue of deceptive techniques in law enforcement.

Impressed by the quality of the debate, the Police Foundation asked Professor Gerald Caplan of the George Washington University Law Center to bring together the best current writings on the issue and edit this volume. We at the Foundation are indebted to Professor Caplan for his excellent work.

Patrick V. Murphy
President
Police Foundation

Introduction

Gerald M. Caplan

Law enforcement agencies have long employed deception as a technique for both detecting crime and apprehending criminals. Undercover agents pretending to be drug buyers, and paid informants spying on associates while purporting to be their friends, are familiar figures. Until recently, use of such agents was largely confined to "vice" offenses such as gambling, prostitution, and narcotics. Lately, however, these intruders have been employed in a very different context: the investigation of elected officials. With the ABSCAM arrests, the Federal Bureau of Investigation surprised us all. ABSCAM was an unprecedented event, a pyrotechnic display, something that could not have happened in J. Edgar Hoover's FBI.

More important, the ABSCAM investigations achieved an immediate popularity. Celebrated by the media, they became the object of widespread imitation by state and local law enforcement and seem likely to be employed with great frequency in the future.

At this date, it is still difficult to come to a conclusion regarding the government's performance in ABSCAM. Dishonest public officials do pose a special threat and FBI Director Webster deserves much credit for taking them on. At the same time, the techniques employed in ABSCAM are peculiarly susceptible to abuse: both innocent individuals and those who, but for the government's enticements, would not have broken the law may get swept up in the investigation.

There is no certain place to fix the line between appropriate and impermissible police conduct, at least if we look to existing law and policy for guidance. Indeed, what is most conspicuous about this area of enforcement is the lack of controlling standards for defining the roles of informants and undercover agents. It is largely unexplored territory.

The seven essays in this collection attempt to map this terrain. They analyze the nature of the criminal conduct involved, the various methods by which it may be detected, and the risks to democratic values at stake. In some cases, the authors go beyond balancing the risks of police techniques against the dangers posed by the unlawful acts, and posit new, alternative approaches in criminal investigation that themselves warrant close study.

The lead essay is an unapologetic defense of the ABSCAM investigations. Its author is Irvin Nathan, the lawyer at the Department of Justice who was in charge of coordinating the prosecutions. Nathan chronicles the events leading up to the arrests of the members of Congress and argues that ABSCAM was a fair and effective method of fighting public corruption. He presents evidence that ABSCAM has operated as a deterrent to others who might betray the public trust.

The specifics of the ABSCAM investigations are put into a broader analytic framework by Professor Mark Moore of the Kennedy School of Government at Harvard University. Professor Moore identifies the special characteristics of "invisible offenses"—those crimes which no victims or witnesses are willing to report to the police—and concludes that undercover operations and the use of informants will continue to be the dominant method of investigation.

Professor Sanford Levinson of the University of Texas College of Law approaches ABSCAM from an entirely different perspective. Levinson argues that undercover operations "lack both an ethical norm and a public policy that takes account of the damage down to the agent, the victim [of police deception], and society." Developing what might be called a morality of betrayal, Levinson presents a typology of informers and an analysis of their behavior in both constitutional—Fourth and Fifth Amendment—and ethical terms.

Sociologist Gary Marx is similarly disturbed by the growth of undercover activities. Marx sees their emergence as an unintended byproduct of recent Supreme Court decisions limiting police powers. As the police use of coercion has been steadily restricted by the Court, their use of deception has increased. Marx examines undercover operations and "stings" from several points of view—the target, the informer, the police, and society in general—and finds them not only of dubious worth, but also a potential threat to democratic ways.

Lawrence W. Sherman, director of research at the Police Foundation and a professor of sociology at the University of Maryland, accepts the view that "deceptive investigative methods pose a tragic choice between equity in law enforcement and the protection of privacy," and proposes an imaginative alternative set of procedures for the police to follow. Sherman proposes a "deductive" method of individual target selection from groups known to have above-average probabilities of committing particular crimes. Each group member would have an equal probability of selection, and target groups would be selected through an open process of administrative rulemaking. Although Sherman's proposal far outruns anything that decisionmakers would be willing to implement in the near future, his ideas do provide a means of safeguarding privacy while at the same time enforcing the law against "invisible" offenses.

Peter Reuter, an economist with the Rand Corporation, is as gloomy about the prospects for controlling police abuse as Sherman is optimistic. Reuter argues, along the lines set by Mark Moore, that "invisible crimes" can be solved only "if the police enter into long-term cooperative relationships with criminals." Drug dealers, he asserts, "who invest a great deal of effort in insulating themselves from dealings with strangers can only be apprehended in many instances if the police enlist the assistance of their confederates." But Reuter departs from Moore and the other contributors by asserting that efforts to control the use of informants are very likely to fail. Accordingly, we must accept a substantial level of misconduct by informants as the price of enforcement, or "we must lower our demands upon the police for the apprehension of certain classes of criminals."

Wayne Kerstetter, formerly a police official with the New York City Department, later superintendent of the Illinois Bureau of Investigation, and now a professor at the University of Illinois at Chicago, offers an "administrative perspective" on undercover operations. Kerstetter shares the insights of a police administrator who has made the tough decisions about target selection and investigative methods. He discusses the trade-offs between the use of deception and of coercion in criminal investigations.

If there is any shortcoming in these essays, it is that the value of ABSCAM-type enterprises are not weighed against a backdrop of reliable data on the scope of official corruption. We do not know enough to balance the dangers of undercover operations to our liberties against the magnitude of the criminality involved. Yet the issue is central. We are willing to give the police more latitude when they deal with serious crime, and are less tolerant of their overzealousness when the offenses investigated are minor. In this regard, we want to know more about ABSCAM. We want to know if the men arrested were more blameworthy than their colleagues who were not subjected to FBI enticements. Are there others in the Congress who peddle themselves on issues that really count—matters of defense or energy or environmental policy? And what does law enforcement know of them?

Clearly, these essays do not answer all the questions. Much remains for future research. But what this collection does offer is significant: the most searching analysis to date of the merits of undercover investigations. As such, they enhance our ability to evaluate police use of deception in the future.

1

ABSCAM: A Fair and Effective Method for Fighting Public Corruption

---

Irvin B. Nathan*

ALL OF THE MAJOR ABSCAM trials having been completed, the time has arrived for an assessment of the operation and an evaluation of the public policy questions of using undercover operations to detect political corruption.

---

* The author was the deputy assistant attorney general in the Department of Justice who coordinated the ABSCAM prosecutions. He is now a partner in a law firm in Washington, D.C. The views expressed herein are the author's alone and are not necessarily the views of the Justice Department or of his law firm.

1

In the series of ABSCAM prosecutions, eight juries in three cities unanimously found guilty of official corruption a senior United States senator; six members of Congress, including the chairmen of two powerful committees in the House; the mayor of Camden, who is also a state senator in New Jersey; the president of the Philadelphia City Council, along with its majority leader and a third member; an inspector for the United States Immigration and Naturalization Service; a Philadelphia lawyer; a New York accountant; and other assorted "business associates" of the public officials. Not one defendant who stood trial was acquitted, although two juries returned verdicts of not guilty on one or two counts.

For the first time in history, a sitting member of Congress, Michael O. Myers of Philadelphia, was expelled from the House of Representatives on the ground of official corruption. Two others, John Jenrette and Raymond Lederer, resigned on the eve of their anticipated expulsion. Five of the six indicted representatives were turned out of office by their constituents when they stood for reelection; only Representative Lederer, whose trial began after the elections, was reelected to his seat, which he vacated after conviction.

Of the 96 jurors, men and women drawn from broad cross-sections of society in Brooklyn, Long Island, Philadelphia, and Washington, D.C., there was not a single holdout. Few of the eight juries required more than a day's deliberation to reach the conclusion that the defendants were guilty beyond a reasonable doubt; most completed their deliberations in a matter of a few hours. In most of the trials, the videotapes were released to the media at the same time they were presented to the juries so that the public could assess the fairness of the juries' verdicts. The unanimity and swiftness of the verdicts reflect the fact-gathering techniques employed by the FBI, the skilled presentation of the evidence by career prosecutors, and the precision with which the charges in the indictments were drafted. They also, of course, reflect the potency of the videotaped capture of a crime in progress.

To date, the appellate courts have been equally unanimous in affirming the ABSCAM jury verdicts. Of four separate panels of appellate courts that have reviewed ABSCAM convictions, three of them have affirmed the convictions unanimously and the U.S. Court of Appeals for the Third Circuit, sitting *en banc,* affirmed the convictions by a 7–2 vote.

2

Each of these courts expressly found that there had been no violation of any defendant's rights under the Constitution and rejected contentions that the government entrapped or otherwise treated the defendants unfairly. As of this writing, the Supreme Court has declined to review the only ABSCAM case to come before it, appeals to intermediate federal appellate courts are pending in two cases and a motion for a new trial is under consideration by a district court in a third case.

By any reckoning, ABSCAM must be considered the most extensive investigation and prosecution of legislative corruption in the nation's history. In no previous federal investigation—not in Watergate, not in Teapot Dome—have so many elected officials at the federal, state and local levels been found guilty and repudiated by their constituents.

The deterrent effect of the operation is not so easily measured, but the evidence of substantial deterrence is clear. In Philadelphia, after the jury verdicts were rendered, the council president pro tem said, "It means that the old politics, backroom politics, darkroom politics, has come to an end. You're going to see the leadership of leaders who are open, more responsive to the people." One need not accept that statement at full value, in Philadelphia or elsewhere, to realize that public officials, aware of such undercover operations, are either going to refrain entirely from such transactions or, at the very least, to be more circumspect in choosing their associates, transactions, and words.

Shortly after the disclosure of ABSCAM, FBI Director William Webster reported that there were more than 50 sophisticated undercover operations underway across the country, involving examinations into various crimes, including public corruption. According to recent testimony by FBI officials, undercover agents in some of these continuing investigations have reported conversations in which suspects attributed their caution to concerns about the possibility of ABSCAM-type probes. This and other evidence suggest that the verdicts of the juries and electorate have been heard and heeded.

Yet the results of the trials and appeals have not stilled the controversy surrounding the techniques employed in the investigation. While jurors and voters have spoken uniformly and unequivocally, questions continue to be raised by defense counsel, commentators, and at least two district court judges about the fairness and propriety of this operation

3

and, more generally, about the future use of undercover operations to ferret out public corruption and white collar crime. Indeed, decisions in each of the cases await judicial review of defendants' post-trial motions, some of which challenge the basic fairness of the ABSCAM operation.

At the heart of the controversy are two questions: How were these public officials selected and what in the future will prevent unscrupulous prosecutors and investigators from employing these techniques to ensnare innocent political enemies? Both questions deserve serious responses.

One indisputable fact must constantly be borne in mind in assessing the fairness of ABSCAM: There was no targeting. There was no hit list. No one in the executive branch, in Washington or elsewhere, ever sat down and selected public officials at whom the ABSCAM operation was to be aimed. All of the public officials who became involved in ABSCAM came into the operation as a result of the representations and actions of corrupt intermediaries. These "bagmen" boasted to people they believed were fellow criminals (but who actually were government agents) about their ability to produce these public officials for illegal actions, sometimes supporting their claims by citing past illegal ventures. The absence of any common thread linking the seven members of Congress found guilty underscores the lack of any governmental selection process. They came from five different states in the East and had widely differing politics, ranging from extreme conservatism to extreme liberalism.

No political official was put off limits; no allegation, regardless of the party, power, or position of the official involved was disregarded as too hot to pursue. When corrupt intermediaries, who had participated in criminal ventures with the undercover operatives, claimed that they could produce a public official to take a bribe, they were invariably invited to live up to their claims. They were told that they would have to produce the allegedly corrupt politician in the flesh and that the politician would have to acknowledge both the bribe and the services to be personally performed for it.

They did fail to produce on a number of occasions, for reasons ranging from outright lies about politicians whom the go-between had never even contacted to a prudent abundance of caution by seemingly predisposed officeholders and their close associates. But the failures were never the result of a veto from a Justice Department representative. As

4

Philip B. Heymann, the head of the Justice Department's Criminal Division, who monitored the investigation and made final prosecutive decisions, testified before a congressional committee, "If a middleman had claimed that he could produce President Carter to take a bribe, we would have swallowed hard but we would not have backed off."

Detractors of ABSCAM attempt to portray an image of high-level Justice Department officials engaged in a crusade against selected public officials or seeking to test the honesty or morality of randomly chosen politicians. The truth of the matter, as shown by the evidence developed in eight public trials, is far different. At critical junctures in the investigation, high-level officials in the Criminal Division and the FBI were faced with essentially only one simple choice: either ignore serious allegations of corruption by refusing to allow contacts with those represented to be ready and willing to engage in criminal conduct, or authorize FBI operatives to pursue the leads they had developed during their investigation, up to and including meeting and offering bribes to public officials identified by proven criminals. It would have been scandalous to have refused to explore fully these serious allegations.

The origins and natural progressions in the ABSCAM investigation have been presented repeatedly in the trials and in congressional hearings. Unfortunately, they apparently have been obscured by the high drama in each case, the videotaped receipt of large amounts of cash by elected officials, often accompanied by such vivid statements as "Money talks, bull shit walks" or "I've got larceny in my blood." Thus, it may be useful to retrace briefly the beginnings and early developments of the operations.

ABSCAM began in the Hauppauge office of the FBI in Long Island in early 1978. Imaginative agents there, headed by group supervisor John Good, began working with a convicted swindler, Melvin Weinberg, who had agreed to cooperate with the government. The scope of the operation was limited at the outset to solving property crimes and recovering stolen or forged securities or art work. The basic setup was simple, and similar to one which Weinberg had run illegally before he had been caught and convicted. Weinberg and agents of the FBI posed as American representatives of fabulously wealthy Arab businessmen interested in shrewd investments in this country, the legality of which did not concern them at all. They created "Abdul Enterprises Limited" (from which the name ABSCAM derived), established an office in Long Island, and spread the word in the netherworld that easy money was available for shady transactions.

As a result of the efforts of Abdul Enterprises, the government was able to recover millions of dollars worth of stolen art and forged stocks, bonds, and certificates of deposit. Private insurance companies paid substantial rewards to Weinberg for his extraordinary efforts in securing return of the stolen works. To this point, there was nothing particularly unusual about the undercover operations, except perhaps the somewhat elaborate cover story. Through the summer of 1978, there was no political orientation to the relatively routine undercover operation.

Things began to change slowly in the fall of 1978, when one of the groups which had previously sold Abdul Enterprises phony certificates of deposit raised a new prospect. They offered to serve as a broker between a New Jersey politician and the fictional Arabs, who had indicated some interest in investing in the newly legalized gambling casinos in Atlantic City. These people described in detail the corrupt relationship they had had with this politician and the influence he claimed he could sell in the state. As a result, the Arabs' representatives met with Angelo Errichetti, the mayor of Camden, New Jersey, who also served as a state senator from New Jersey. In short order, Errichetti and the undercover operatives developed a profoundly corrupt relationship.

In the spring of 1979, Errichetti furnished the FBI operatives, still believing them to be agents of the wealthy and unscrupulous Arab sheiks, with a written list of names of those who he claimed were corrupt federal and state politicians in and around New Jersey. He claimed he could put the operatives in touch with these allegedly corrupt politicians should the need arise. In the course of his continuing dealings with the operatives, Errichetti soon had an opportunity to fulfill his boast.

In late July 1979, aboard a yacht in Florida, a meeting was held with Errichetti and others to discuss a proposed casino transaction. Also present at the meeting were people whom Errichetti had introduced to the FBI operatives as instrumental in the casino deal, including Louis Johanson, a Philadelphia city council member, and his law partner Howard Criden. During the cruise, the glib and extremely effective undercover FBI agent Anthony Amoroso, posing as Tony DeVito, the Arabs' righthand man, remarked that the sheiks might have to flee their country and seek asylum in the United States. He said that the sheiks did not want to face a situation like the one that had confronted Anastasio Somoza, the deposed Nicaraguan leader, who had been expelled from this country shortly after his arrival. Amoroso did not suggest how this problem might be avoided. Errichetti and Criden took the initiative and embarked on a campaign of lining up members of Congress who, in return for cash, would take actions to guarantee asylum for the fictional sheiks. This was, in essence, the beginning of the congressional phase of ABSCAM.

To this point the Department of Justice in Washington had very limited involvement in the development of ABSCAM. Even more important, at this time, in late July 1979, the FBI and Justice personnel had no designs on any officials and had probably not even heard of Ozzie Myers, Raymond Lederer, or Richard Kelly.

The first mention of the names of Representatives Myers and Lederer was made by Errichetti on July 29, 1979, when he claimed that he had lined them up to meet with the sheiks' representatives in order to provide immigration assistance. In subsequent conversations, Errichetti said that the price for each would be $100,000. Weinberg later got the price reduced to $50,000.

Thus, when this phase of the ABSCAM case came to Washington, the question was whether the agents would be authorized to offer and pay $50,000 bribes to Representatives Myers and Lederer, two public officials whom Mayor Errichetti represented as ready and willing to sell their offices for that amount. The decision Director Webster faced, in consultation with the head of the Criminal Division, was whether to authorize the agents to proceed or whether to call them off. If the director had disapproved the request, the serious allegations raised against two sitting congressmen would never have been proven or refuted. In effect, the allegations would have been covered up. By authorizing the approach, the director gave the named representatives an opportunity to clear themselves or to incriminate themselves. No conscientious law enforcement official could have made any other decision.

7

The ground rules communicated to all the FBI operatives were designed to thwart unscrupulous middlemen and eliminate any ambiguity. The operatives were directed to make it clear that the representatives themselves would be required to appear, would be told unequivocally what was expected of them and would have to accept or acknowledge receipt of the bribe. Every meeting between the operatives and a member of Congress at which a bribe was offered or passed was videotaped. These videotapes are there for all to see and to determine whether these conditions were met, whether the mutual exchanges of promises were unambiguous and whether the public officials were pressured or fooled in any way. The juries had no trouble with these questions.

Either Errichetti or Criden or both were involved in the introductions to Representatives Myers, Lederer, Thompson, and Murphy. Indeed, it was Thompson who first raised Murphy's name and then introduced the operatives to him for a corrupt transaction. The same pattern held in the cases of Representatives Jenrette and Kelly. In each case, an intermediary claimed to be able to produce a legislator who, in return for cash, would be willing to assist in the immigration problems. In all cases, the names and predispositions were first raised by the intermediaries who had no reason to believe that they were dealing with the government and who had little incentive to lie.

In all of the cases, except that involving Jenrette, the intermediaries were told of the supposed immigration problems *before* they disclosed which members of Congress they could produce to lend assistance in return for a bribe. In the Jenrette case, the FBI operatives had been dealing with a South Carolina businessman, John Stowe, on a deal involving forged certificates of deposit. In the course of those discussions, Stowe said that he knew a representative who was "as big a crook as I am" and would assist in the certificates of deposit transaction. Stowe identified the legislator as John Jenrette. After the securities deal fell through, the operatives asked Stowe whether he thought Jenrette would be willing to assist in the immigration problem in return for cash. Stowe reported that Jenrette was interested and the meetings and the payoff to Jenrette ensued.

The case involving Senator Williams proceeded along a slightly different track, but the pattern was essentially the same. The testimony in the Williams trial showed that after Mayor Errichetti learned of the enormous wealth of the Arabs and their eagerness to seek political influence in this country, Errichetti communicated his find to Senator Williams. The senior senator from New Jersey then immediately directed his long-time associate, Alex Feinberg, to have Errichetti put Feinberg in touch with the Arab representatives. Feinberg advised the sheiks' agents of Senator Williams's interest in a titanium mine and of the urgent need for substantial financing. As a result, Senator Williams met repeatedly, face-to-face, with the undercover agents, promising to use his influence with the president of the United States, the vice president, the secretaries of defense and state, and others to secure government purchases of titanium from the mine in return for a $100-million loan.

Of course, the government had set the bait by having its undercover agents tell the corrupt intermediaries they were willing to pay for political influence. But the government had no idea which politicians would rise to the bait and made no effort to push the bait toward any particular public officials. Neither had the government any idea which of the politicians was in fact corrupt and which was not. The process was very similar to the ordinary undercover fencing operation, in which government agents spread the word that they are willing to purchase stolen property at a discount for ready cash. At the time the operation is set up and the word goes out, the agents have no idea which people are going to come in with stolen goods. The agents take all comers, whether it be the town's most notorious thief or its minister. Similarly, in ABSCAM, it would have been improper for the government to close up shop when, instead of two-bit con men, the names of powerful public officials were raised as ready and willing to deal.

It is also untrue that law enforcement officials were running around Washington "offering bribes, willy-nilly, in hopes someone" would accept something, as at least one newspaper editorial charged. Whether or not it would be unfair or improper to offer a bribe to randomly selected public officials, who like many others must face similar temptations every day, it would be an extremely imprudent and wasteful expenditure of scarce law enforcement resources. How could one justify the time and effort to go on a wild goose chase with no prospects of success? This was not done in ABSCAM, and it is unlikely that any law enforcement administrator, in the face of rising crime rates and reduced budgets and staff, would do so. As in ABSCAM, law enforcement officials will not devote resources unless they have been alerted to the dangers of a serious crime problem in the area, even if they do not know the particular culprits involved.

Some critics argue that the government should have solid evidence, something approaching probable cause, to believe a particular public official has engaged in similar illegal conduct in the past before a bribe can be offered. Such a requirement would be unreasonable, unnecessary, and unworkable.

Consider the analogy of the "granny squads" which are common in urban police forces. When a particular park or downtown street is plagued with muggings and other violent crime, police may disguise themselves as vulnerable elderly women with handbags ready to be snatched. When the disguised police officers enter the crime area, neither they nor their colleagues in waiting have any idea who is going to try to rip them off. Thereafter, if the scenario goes as planned, a thug appears, grabs the purse, attempts to run off, and is captured. Only later do the police learn whether this thief has a record. While the existence of a record may make some difference with respect to ultimate punishment, it should make no difference with respect to whether or not the thief should be prosecuted.

Substitute a member of Congress taking a bribe and ask what difference should it make at the investigative stage whether the government can prove that this politician had ever before taken a bribe. The question is will he or she, as represented, engage in illegality on this occasion under circumstances that closely approximate the real world. For the government to undertake a full-scale investigation into the alleged previous incidents before a fast-breaking transaction is consummated would be time-consuming and not particularly worthwhile. In responding to the proffered bribe, the public official can either prove or disprove the outstanding allegation without any reference to previous behavior. Even first offenders should be prosecuted. It seems likely that those who would be caught in decoy transactions—whether it is ripping off "grannies" or taking bribes—are those who are likely to have engaged in such conduct in the past.

Further, in considering whether to pursue the allegations raised by corrupt intermediaries, the government had to consider the source of the allegations and the likelihood that they were telling the truth. If a total stranger were to come into the police station and make an allegation of corruption against a public official, the allegation should, of course, be fully explored, even if there is a substantial chance that the allegation is a fabrication. There could be many reasons why this person may be fabricating the story, but no self-respecting investigator or prosecutor would ignore the allegation. How then could the investigators in ABSCAM have failed to pursue allegations coming from people with whom they had dealt reliably in the past?

The intermediaries had every reason to tell the truth to the Arabs' representatives. First, they had established continuing corrupt relationships with them and presumably desired to continue the relationships so long as they proved profitable. If their information proved unreliable, the relationship, along with the anticipated reward, would be damaged or destroyed. Second, they were advised that they would have to produce the public officials for blatant offers of bribes. There would, of course, be considerable embarrassment if, at the meeting, the public official were to protest complete ignorance about the transaction and storm out. This would jeopardize the intermediary's status with both the public official and with the Arabs' representatives. Bringing an innocent public official to such a meeting would involve the risk that the official would inform the authorities, leading to the possibility of prosecution and to retribution from the Arabs' representatives—a risk not lightly run. Indeed, no public official brought to a meeting in ABSCAM ever reported a bribe offer to any law enforcement agency.

Another source of concern for some of ABSCAM's critics is the question of entrapment. This concern is based on the clearly correct notion that it is unfair to trap or trick innocent persons into taking illegal action they had no previous inclination to pursue. The law of entrapment is well settled. When this defense is raised by a defendant who essentially admits engaging in the illegal transaction, the jury must decide whether the accused was ready and willing to commit the crime if an opportunity should be presented or whether a person not otherwise predisposed to wrongdoing was corrupted by some overreaching or special inducement.

11

The focus in this defense is properly on the mental state of the defendant, and it is provable or rebuttable by many different factors, including the prior conduct and words of the defendant, his or her knowledge before engaging in the criminal act, the alacrity with which he or she enters into the criminal act, the language and body movements accompanying the commission of the criminal act, and actions and relationships to the others involved after the commission of the criminal act. It is an individual defense and one which must be passed upon by the jury based on particular facts presented to it.

Curiously, although entrapment is often mentioned in the press, and even though words like "traps" and "snares" were thrown about in court by defense counsel, very few of the defendants actually raised the formal defense of entrapment. In each case where it was raised, the jury rejected the defense. In only one case did a judge disturb the jury's verdict. In a Philadelphia case involving two city council members, the court was not satisfied with the evidence of predisposition and set aside the guilty verdicts. That decision was reversed by the U.S. Court of Appeals for the Third Circuit sitting *en banc*.

Eschewing the entrapment defense, many of those prosecuted raised novel and bizarre defenses. For example, Representative Myers did not claim that he was pressured or coerced into taking $50,000 in $100 bills or into demanding an additional $85,000. Instead, his defense was that he was "play acting," only pretending that he would introduce legislation or take other acts to guarantee asylum while ripping off "fat-cat" Arabs. Representative Kelly, a former state judge from Florida, contended that when he took the $25,000 and stuffed it in his pockets, it was only part of his own investigation, an investigation which he never bothered to document or report to anyone else. The principal defense raised by Representative Jenrette, who also claimed entrapment, was that he was in a state of incapacitating inebriation for several months before and after his demand for and receipt of $50,000 and therefore should not be held accountable for his actions. It is striking to contrast these defenses with the simultaneous requests by these men to their constituents that they be returned to positions of high trust.

Entrapment was rarely raised, and was never accepted by a jury, for a very simple reason: there was none. No pressure was brought to bear on any public official; there was no badgering, no intimidation, no coercion, no imploring, no pandering. Judge Jon Newman, who previously served as a top aide to a senior United States senator, spoke for a unanimous panel of the Second Circuit Court of Appeals when, in rejecting an argument that ABSCAM represented an unconstitutional abuse, he made the unanswerable observation: "Any member of Congress approached by agents conducting a bribery sting operation can simply say 'No.'" Any of the seven members of Congress was free to turn down the proposition, leave the room, and report the matter to the FBI. None of them did so.

Courts have developed the entrapment defense to protect unsophisticated people who could be lured or pressured into criminality without a clear appreciation of the consequences of their actions. It is farfetched to suggest that members of Congress—some of whom had held their seats for more than 20 years—were so naive or impressionable that they could be tricked or trapped into doing something that they were not predisposed to do. It was the Congress which had determined that this conduct should be deemed criminal in the first place.

During the eight trials, all of the interaction between the government operatives and the public officials was presented to the juries on videotapes without any editing. Every statement, every blandishment, every facial expression, every body movement by all of the participants was there in plain sight for the juries to consider. If a single one of the 96 jurors had thought that the government's conduct was high-handed, overreaching, or otherwise unfair to the public officials, he or she could have voted to acquit. Yet not a single one indicated by his or her vote a belief that there was any unfairness in the ABSCAM operation.

For the future, the tougher question is whether the public can be assured that these techniques will not be abused by unscrupulous and unethical executive branch officials against their political enemies in the legislative branch. The short answer is that any effective law enforcement tool can, in the wrong hands, be abused, but that is no reason to eliminate or outlaw the technique. Further, the dangers of abuse can be reduced by establishing and adhering to certain guiding principles and by continuing to have close judicial scrutiny, aided by vigilant defense counsel, after an operation is completed.

13

Actually the dangers of abuse are greatly exaggerated because the consensual bribe scenario is a very unlikely and unpromising technique to use against political adversaries. It is unlikely to be used because it requires the agreement and cooperation of the target. As the unanimous panel of the Second Circuit recognized, "Each member's capacity to reject bribe opportunities could be regarded as sufficient safeguard against the risks that the executive branch would successfully use these tactics for political reprisals." There are a number of non-consensual devices which unscrupulous prosecutors would be far more likely to use if they wanted to incriminate falsely an innocent legislator. For example, contraband could be planted or, as in the celebrated case several years ago involving George Ratterman, an innocent person could be drugged or intoxicated and then photographed in compromising positions. Even without taking these dramatic steps, unscrupulous individuals out to smear opponents could simply publish unconfirmed reports from raw investigative files. Such odious measures would be far easier and more reliable methods for the unscrupulous than an elaborate bribery sting operation, which requires the participation of a large number of people, and, in the end, depends for its success on the willingness and criminal intent of the target.

Of course, the basic issue is the integrity and decency of the prosecutors and investigators. No such federal sting could be run without the active cooperation and support of the attorney general, the deputy attorney general, the director of the FBI, and the assistant attorney general in charge of the Criminal Division. Each of these presidential appointees is subject to Senate review and confirmation. All of those who held these positions during ABSCAM were honorable people who would not have participated in or condoned any chicanery. Moreover, an operation like ABSCAM requires the combined efforts of dozens of career agents and prosecutors. It is far-fetched to believe, especially in this day and age, that they would go along with any operation that deliberately attempted to ensnare innocent targets. The whistle would be blown promptly on any such proposal.

In the future, any sophisticated federal undercover operation will be conducted under a detailed set of guidelines, promulgated in January 1981 by outgoing Attorney General Civiletti. The guidelines, which for

14

the most part set forth the principles followed in ABSCAM, establish elaborate review procedures within the Department of Justice and mandate certain criteria designed to minimize any possibility of entrapment or other unfairness to potential defendants. The guidelines require that no such operation can be approved unless there is a reasonable indication that the individual has engaged or is engaging in the contemplated illegal activity or that only those predisposed would be expected to enter the operation. Further, the guidelines require that the proposed operation be "based solely on the law enforcement considerations." In addition, the details of the operation must satisfy the reviewing board that:

(A) the corrupt nature of the activity is reasonably clear to potential subjects;

(B) there is reasonable indication that the undercover operation will reveal illegal activities; and

(C) the nature of any inducement is not unjustifiable in view of the character of the illegal transaction in which the individual is invited to engage.

The essence of the guidelines is to make sure that the opportunities for crime resemble those in the real world as closely as possible and to make sure that the illegal nature of the opportunity is unambiguous. In the real world, most people—whether they be bank tellers, lawyers, domestics, bookkeepers or legislators—are faced with temptations and opportunities almost daily. If the opportunities presented by a sting operation are commensurate with those faced regularly by a public official, there is no element of unfairness in prosecuting him or her for having willfully seized it. Actually, this is an area in which fairness and practicality coalesce. If the circumstances are not similar to those found in the real world—for example, if the proffered rewards are too large or the pressures too overbearing, juries will not convict and judges will not sustain convictions.

Finally, the most basic safeguards are trial and appellate courts. In the end, the courts must scrutinize the evidence to determine whether there is any credible proof that an operation was directed at political opponents or whether it was in any other way fundamentally unfair to the defendants. Fortunately, in this electronic era, courts will be able to rely, in large measure, on audio and videotaped reproductions of the pivotal events to rule on any allegations of government overreaching or other misconduct.

When courts determine the fundamental fairness of these operations, they should compare, among other things, the quality of evidence in such videotaped operations with, for example, the testimony of a disaffected participant in an alleged bribe transaction committed years earlier by a prominent public official of theretofore unblemished reputation. They should also consider the likelihood that there will ever be a report of a bribe between two consenting individuals, each of whom has profited from the transaction. The court should also consider whether an operation such as ABSCAM is not less intrusive and less coercive than other judicially sanctioned techniques. They should compare the consensually recorded conversations between public officials and strangers to court-ordered wiretaps and bugs, where no party to the conversation knows that it is being overheard or recorded; judicially issued search warrants executed in private homes and offices against the wills of the owners; and grand jury or trial testimony compelled against friends or even relatives. All that the undercover technique relies upon is the willingness of public officials to engage in criminal conduct and make damaging admissions voluntarily and intentionally to those they believe are colleagues in crime. They recognize, of course, the risk that at some later date these people could reveal damaging information to the authorities, but they believe either that this is a remote possibility or that if a case is brought they will be able to put their credibility on the line against these criminal actors. What they do not know is that their voluntary words or actions are being recorded and are available for future use against them.

When all of these factors are considered, it becomes apparent that sophisticated undercover operations are fair and effective and represent the wave of the future in combatting public corruption as well as a variety of other consensual crimes. I suggest that this is good news, at least for law-abiding citizens.

2

Invisible Offenses:
A Challenge to Minimally
Intrusive Law Enforcement

Mark H. Moore*

LAW ENFORCEMENT IN A FREE society must strike a delicate balance between protecting individual rights to privacy (especially from government-sponsored surveillance) and the society's interest in detecting

* This paper was originally prepared for presentation at a conference on deceptive enforcement techniques sponsored by the Hastings Institute and held at Harvard University on April 16–17, 1981. The paper is part of a continuing collaborative research effort between the author and Professor Philip B. Heymann of the Harvard Law School. In addition, the author has benefited from the able assistance of Michael Bromwich, Brenda Gruss, and Laurence Latourette. I acknowledge these contributions not to share blame for errors, but to ensure that any virtues of the paper are credited to those who created them.

criminal offenses and punishing offenders.[1] Often this tension is seen as one between a *principled* defense of civil liberties and a mere *utilitarian* interest in reducing crime. In this formulation, the protection of civil liberties seems the nobler cause. It is tempting, therefore, to resolve issues concerning enforcement policies and methods by appeal to constitutionally based principles guarding civil liberties.[2]

Undoubtedly, there is wisdom in looking first to constitutional principles for guidance in regulating enforcement strategies. But reliance on constitutional principles guarding individual privacy as the touchstone for enforcement policy is insufficient. In important areas of enforcement activity such as informants, undercover operations, and grand jury investigations, constitutional principles leave, perhaps, too much latitude to enforcement agencies.[3] Moreover, the society has more at stake in the design of enforcement strategies than the protection of individual privacy from government scrutiny. As a matter of principle, for example, we should assure the overall rationality and fairness of enforcement strategies.[4] This means that enforcement efforts should be directed toward serious offenses, not wasted on trivial matters. It also means that, holding the nature of the offense constant, the risks of investigation, effective prosecution, and punishment should be approximately equal among criminal offenders. Or, somewhat less restrictively, the risks should be independent of the social position or sophistication of the offender, as well as of any special hostility of enforcement agencies.[5] Finally, we can reasonably be interested in preventing criminal offenses and promoting social order at the least possible cost. To the extent that constitutional principles are silent or ambiguous in important areas, and to the extent that other social interests deserve to be recognized and accommodated in designing enforcement strategies, it is necessary to take the design (or evaluation) of enforcement strategies out of the realm of purely constitutional issues and place the enterprise in the more ambiguous realm of social policy, where diverse values compete without a clear hierarchy.[6]

Viewed from this perspective, the tensions in the design of enforcement strategies are more apparent. We would like to detect and solve crimes, but we don't want to intrude in private areas or field a massive enforcement bureaucracy. We would like our enforcement efforts to be fair among offenders, but interests in non-intrusiveness and economy prevent us from positioning public agencies to note and respond to all offenses, thereby creating the potential for systematic biases in enforcement operations.

As is often the case, we have solved this tangle of competing interests not through explicit discussion, but through the evolution of an enforcement strategy that seems to balance the interests rather nicely. Essentially, the solution leaves most of the burden of detecting and investigating criminal offenses to private individuals.[7] As part of this strategy, we have established legal doctrines and enforcement procedures that restrict public investigative activities to *reactions* to criminal offenses.[8] In our conception, the public interest in controlling crime and punishing offenders overwhelms a general interest in protecting privacy only when an offense occurs or becomes imminent. Moreover, we imagine that enforcement agencies learn of such offenses not by positioning themselves in every nook and cranny of the society, but through private individuals who come forward to tell the agency about the offense, or through relatively superficial and visible patrol measures.

By limiting efforts to detect offenses to private mobilization and visible patrol activities, we solve the problem of detecting offenses in an inexpensive and non-intrusive way. Moreover, there is an appearance of full and impartial enforcement of the law because all allegations from citizens receive a certain amount of investigative activity, and because the patrol activity, although relatively superficial, is nonetheless fairly distributed over the space within which offenses might occur. Thus, by relying on private mobilization, a broad but superficial patrol activity, and investigative apparatus activated only when a crime has occurred, we create an enforcement apparatus that minimizes government threats to individual civil liberties, is inexpensive to operate, and appears fair in its application of the law.[9]

This strategy of enforcement seems to work well in terms of controlling crime and promoting security as long as we think of crimes such as robbery, rape, and assault, and as long as we think of apprehending offenders after the fact rather than trying to prevent these offenses. In such situations, it is plausible that victims and witnesses, motivated by nothing more than a sense of injustice, will come forward to say that an offense has occurred, and assist the police in identifying and apprehending the offender. Of course, some difficulties arise when the motives of witnesses seem tainted, or, as in many domestic quarrels and barroom brawls, when it is difficult to distinguish the offender from the victim. Still, for many important offenses, the reactive strategy for deploying enforcement effort seems to work well.

Problems with this conception arise, however, when we try to enforce against offenses for which no victims and witnesses are willing to report that an offense has occurred, or when we try to thwart specific crimes before they occur. For such activities the reactive strategy may be inappropriate, and some different principles of enforcement action must be brought to bear.

The purpose of this chapter is to explore the wisdom of departing from the traditional reactive strategy of enforcement and engaging in more aggressive *proactive* strategies for more or less limited purposes. The argument is that some important criminal offenses are largely invisible to traditional enforcement methods and, consequently, that if we relied solely on traditional methods, offenders committing these offenses would be relatively immune to effective prosecution. This not only creates a nagging weakness, but also introduces an important inequity into our system of enforcement. The only way to shore up enforcement against these invisible offenses is to rely on enforcement strategies that are much more intrusive than the traditional methods; for example, covert surveillance, heavier reliance on informants, the use of undercover operations to instigate offenses, and so on. Interests in enhancing the equity and overall effectiveness of enforcement strategies will, therefore, counsel the use of these techniques against invisible offenses despite the risks to individual privacy. But these intrusive techniques can also be effective against traditional offenses. If that is true, and if we are not barred *in principle* from using the techniques, then perhaps they should be used in enforcing against traditional crimes as well. And, indeed, the more we think about these alternative approaches, the less obviously inferior they seem to reliance on the whims and caprices of private individuals who do most of the actual policing in our current system. Thus, the existence of invisible offenses and the specialized patrolling and investigative strategies

20

for dealing with them challenge our conventional thinking about the best way to balance competing social interests in the design of enforcement strategies.

Invisible Offenses

By now, we are all familiar with the idea of victimless crimes.[10] We understand that for narcotics offenses, vice offenses, gambling, and so on, we lack an indignant victim to assist police investigations. There may be indignant witnesses, of course, and they may mobilize the police, but the witnesses can rarely establish convincingly that a crime occurred and the police arrive too late to see the crime in progress. To enforce effectively against such offenses, then, we have been forced to rely on a variety of measures that depend crucially on deception. We encourage covert physical surveillance of areas where such activity is suspected; we recruit informants to tell us when and where offenses are likely to occur and who is involved; and we organize undercover operations to instigate offenses.[11] Since these enforcement methods extend the scope of government surveillance and involve the government in suspect acts and relationships; the offenses do not seem all that serious and, indeed, are plausibly inconsistent with the proper use of government authority in a liberal state; and little effective deterrence seems to result; the enforcement of laws against victimless crimes seems to many a bad bargain. The jurisprudential lesson typically drawn from this analysis is that it is a mistake to legislate personal morality.[12]

If we looked at these offenses from a slightly different perspective, however, and understood that from an investigative point of view the problem with these offenses was not that they legislated morality, but that they deprived investigators of the focus and assistance provided by victims and witnesses, then we would see that at least three other kinds of offenses posed similar difficulties.

One kind produces victims but the victims do not notice that they have been victimized because the effects are broadly diffused or occur far in the future. White-collar offenses such as tax evasion and counterfeiting fall within this class. So does bribery, where inappropriate uses of public authority fail to produce a cognizant victim. Among offenses that produce effects far in the future are the illegal disposal of toxic wastes, the embezzlement of pension funds, and the sale of phony securities to people with long-term savings plans.

A second sort of offense produces victims, and the victims know they have been victimized, but, for a variety of reasons, the victims are reluctant to come forward. The most obvious offenses here are extortionate crimes—protection rackets, loansharking, blackmail, or simply extortion. Less obvious are ordinary crimes of violence or exploitation carried on in the context of a continuing relationship in which one individual is much more powerful than the other. Spouse abuse, child abuse, and sexual harassment by employers or landlords are examples of these sorts of offenses. It is important to note that obstructing justice by intimidating witnesses falls into this category as well.[13] In fact, the intimidation of witnesses could make many ordinary street offenses, ones that should, in principle, be easy for the government to observe, invisible.

A third class of offenses will produce victims, but has not done so because they have not yet occurred. The most obvious offenses here are violations of laws that make preparing or attempting to commit offenses a crime. Conspiracy laws provide the most salient example. In addition, some acts are made crimes not because they indicate preparation, but simply because they are statistically related to future harms that are criminal. To a degree, laws against speeding, drunk driving, and perhaps even public drunkenness can be understood as efforts to prevent criminal offenses. Finally, there is an intermediate category of offense where the acts lie between conscious preparation for criminal offenses and acts that are statistically linked to the probability that a criminal offense will occur. Illegal possession or carrying of weapons, possession of burglar's tools, and possession of narcotics paraphernalia are examples of these sorts of offenses.

What all of these offenses have in common is that there is no victim willing to indicate that an offense has been committed and assist in the identification of the offender. There may be witnesses, but the witnesses are apt to be co-conspirators, or people who find themselves reluctant to come forward for the same reasons as the victims. From the point of view of most private citizens, and therefore the government, then, the offenses are largely invisible. Or, more precisely, for any given level of enforcement effort, these offenses will be detected less commonly than offenses that leave indignant victims, outraged witnesses, and scattered physical clues in their wake.

Enforcement Strategies and Intrusiveness

The central problem in enforcing against invisible offenses is that no private individual is motivated to sound an alarm that an offense has occurred, or to assist public agencies in identifying and apprehending the offender. To deal with such offenses, then, we must find some special ways of motivating victims to assist us, or of positioning enforcement agents to observe and report on the offenses. In effect, we must create publicly sponsored substitutes for privately motivated victims and witnesses. Inevitably, the efforts to encourage victims and witnesses or to position agents to observe the invisible offenses will be more objectionable than enforcement efforts designed primarily to react to clearly visible offenses. The question, of course, is how intrusive various enforcement methods are. To answer that question, we need to be a little more precise about the concept of intrusiveness.

As we think about the idea of intrusiveness in the context of enforcement activities, it seems that it can be calibrated in at least six dimensions. One dimension is simply how *extensive* the government surveillance is; that is, how large a piece of the world is subject to some degree of government surveillance. In setting limits on the scope of government information gathering, our legal tradition has marked out spheres that are specially deserving of protection from government surveillance because they are linked to conditions necessary for private autonomy or effective political expression: private spaces such as houses and offices are protected from government surveillance more rigorously than public spaces such as commercial establishments and streets;[14] some relationships such as lawyer-client, doctor-patient, husband-wife are considered sancrosanct while others (such as mere friendship) are less reliably protected from government intrusion;[15] speech and conversation are protected more carefully than records of transactions, and records are protected more than behavior in public locations. To the extent that government information gathering crosses these barriers and intrudes into ever more intimate areas, it may be thought of as becoming more extensive—of reaching more areas of activity than we ordinarily expect.

A second dimension of intrusiveness is how *intensive* the surveillance becomes. This dimension is concerned not with the size and kinds of spaces that are vulnerable to some degree of government surveillance, but instead with how deeply or thoroughly the spaces are explored. A cop on every corner would be experienced as intrusive by most citizens, not because official surveillance had moved into previously well defended areas, but because it has reached a high degree of intensiveness with respect to a traditional area. Similarly, an extensive search of a house or office by a squad of police officers armed with sledgehammers would probably be experienced as more intrusive than a casual examination of one's desk by a single detective, even if both searches were covered by a warrant justifying the intrusion into ordinarily private areas. Our ordinary expectations that the government's information-gathering efforts will be limited by scarce resources as well as legal protections cause us to feel intruded upon by unusual thoroughness in information gathering, even when the government surveillance meets all legal requirements. In effect, expectations of privacy, which is the constitutional bulwark in deciding what is tolerable and what not, are defined by common knowledge of the resources available to the police as well as by legal guarantees.[16]

Note that resource constraints impose a natural balance between the extensiveness of government information gathering and its intensiveness. A rational enforcement enterprise (mindful of its obligations to solve crimes at low cost) would not willingly spend its resources searching in areas where the likelihood of finding a crime or a criminal was very low. Instead, it would concentrate on areas where crimes and criminals were very likely to be found. In this respect, the economizing interests of enforcement agencies parallel a legal interest in assuring that some justification can be given for focusing unusually extensive and intensive information gathering in a limited area. The predicate established for unusual levels of enforcement activity, or the probable cause required for government searches, has the effect of marking out a limited area of social life that is unusually likely to contain a criminal offense, and thereby both justify and limit intensive government information gathering. This is in

24

the interests of both minimally intrusive and inexpensive law enforcement methods.

A third feature of enforcement strategies linked to perceived intrusiveness is the extent to which the information gathering is *focused on persons* (or classes of persons) rather than on times, places, or activities. Ordinarily, government information gathering is organized around acts: the government seeks to position itself so it can observe criminal activity, or it seeks to discover how a past act occurred. As a practical matter, we could try to find criminal acts by watching people as they moved through the social environment as well as by trying to pick out pieces of the social environment particularly likely to contain crimes. For example, we could trail known muggers as well as watch the areas around subway stops, or we could rely on "profiles" describing typical characteristics of drug smugglers as well as using particular itineraries or nervousness in preliminary inspections to trigger more thorough searches. In fact, if a few people committed many crimes and did so in very unpredictable times and places, it would probably be more efficient to organize surveillance and information gathering around the people rather than the acts: that is, we could do better both in controlling crime and in minimizing government intrusion.

Despite this possibility, however, tradition regards surveillance organized around persons (particularly suspect classes of persons) as more dangerous to civil liberties than similar levels of surveillance organized around places or activities in which the people being observed are anonymous. The justification for making this distinction is probably that expectations of anonymity are closely tied to privacy interests. Combining pieces of information about an individual strips away privacy much more quickly and thoroughly than simply making the observations and leaving them unrelated to individuals.[17] Another justification may be that focusing on persons has the potential of reflecting, or even stimulating, improper *ad hominem* motivations within the government information-gathering enterprise. We are more capable of feeling angry and vicious about people whom we regard as reprehensible than we are of feeling passionate about discrete acts. Thus, a focus on acts helps to banish atavistic passions from our enforcement efforts.

A fourth feature of government information-gathering techniques that affects the perceived degree of intrusiveness is the role of *deception* or disguise. In general, the use of disguised or deceptive surveillance dramatically increases the felt "extensiveness" of government information gathering. This occurs for at least two reasons. First, the general guarantees to citizens about the extensiveness and intensiveness of government surveillance tend to become less certain. After all, deceptive techniques can intrude into very private areas. If the government is allowed to recruit informants from among one's friends, or to place electronic devices in one's home or office, or to insinuate an undercover operation into a business relationship by establishing phony credentials, then one must feel vulnerable even in areas that were well defended. Moreover, because the techniques are secret, the public lacks reliable information about how commonly and widely they are used. Thus, it is hard for the public to form reasonable views about how likely it is that they are under surveillance at any given time. If everyone exaggerates risks in situations of uncertainty, the effect of deceptive techniques will be to amplify public fears about the extent of government surveillance. Second, not only will the most general guarantees totter, but the capacity of the citizens to determine at any given moment whether they are under surveillance will also weaken. Deception means that citizens can no longer rely on what they see around them to help them form judgments about whether they are under observation or investigation.[18] They must keep in mind that they might be under surveillance even when there is nothing in the environment that suggests that this is true. Of course, there may be many other reasons to object to the government's use of disguise and deception. For example, it may be morally wrong in itself. But what is being argued here is that one of the reasons that governments might choose not to engage in deception is that it inevitably magnifies the perceived intrusiveness of government surveillance.

A fifth dimension of government information gathering associated with intrusiveness is government efforts to *enlist victims and witnesses* in making cases against defendants. Many government activities in this area are unobjectionable—even virtuous. The offer of protection to witnesses who feel afraid, the willingness to schedule court hearings to accommodate the schedules of victims and witnesses, the provision of

26

counseling and support services to rape victims, and so on, all seem tolerable. If anything, such measures seem to protect the capacity of the victim or witness to play his or her appropriate role in the criminal justice system. But other ways of attracting support, such as offering rewards, guaranteeing anonymity, dropping criminal charges against potential witnesses, and so on, seem more troublesome. The reason is that such actions confound our understanding of the motivations of the victim and witnesses. These people have the greatest credibility when they have nothing at stake in the outcome of a case other than an interest in justice. If that is their only motivation, we can feel more confident that they are telling the truth. If, on the other hand, there is something else at stake, such as a reward or a diminished penalty, then we are less confident that the person is truthful. It is hard to know exactly when the government's efforts to allow people to say what they know shades into efforts to persuade them to say things that they do not know. Worries about this phenomenon make government efforts to "recruit" victims and witnesses seem threatening and intrusive.

In fact, there is one special way that the government recruits witnesses and victims to cooperate that deserves special recognition because it depends exclusively on the coercive power of the state. That is the use of grand juries to compel testimony (on pain of jail sentences for contempt of court) from immunized witnesses.[19] In the amount and kind of state power employed, grand juries represent broad powers to reach into the social arrangements surrounding offenders, victims, witnesses, and their associates.

A sixth dimension of investigative techniques that raises civil liberties concerns is government's involvement in *instigating* (as opposed to merely observing) criminal offenses.[20] Note that the instigation could involve undercover agents whose salaries are paid entirely by the government, or informants recruited for a short-run purpose. The difference between instigation and passive observation is that, in instigation, the government agent plays a role in encouraging the offense to occur. The agents offer themselves as victims to muggers in the park, or buy illegal drugs, or provide some of the information or materials that offenders might need to commit an offense. It is obvious that instigation always depends on deception: the government informant or employee must

27

disguise his or her real position and intentions. Thus, all the intrusive features associated with covert information gathering is inherent in instigation as well. In addition, however, instigation is in some sense coercive: it tempts offenders into committing crimes that they might otherwise not have committed.[21] As in the case of government efforts to recruit witnesses, the government's role in helping the crime to occur confounds our interpretation of the crime. The offender's motivation and willingness to commit the offense remain uncertain because of the government's complicity. No doubt, there is a continuum ranging from passive observation through very minor and easily duplicable sorts of "assistance" the government provides, to large and unique contributions by the government. Exactly where one crosses a line on that continuum that makes government actions intolerably intrusive remains both unclear and unjustified. Nevertheless, that government intrusiveness increases as one moves along that complex continuum is fairly well agreed.

In sum, the intrusiveness of government enforcement strategies can usefully be characterized in six dimensions linked to civil liberties and due process concerns: 1) the *extensiveness* of the effort (how large a piece of social activity is exposed to government surveillance, and how many boundaries marking especially private areas are crossed); 2) the *intensiveness* of the effort (how thoroughly the areas under observation are observed); 3) whether the focus is on *persons* or on time, place, and activity; 4) the *covertness or deceptiveness* of the information gathering; 5) the size and character of *inducements offered to witnesses* or victims of offenses; and 6) the government's role in *instigating or facilitating the offense*. The overall intrusiveness of a given enforcement strategy depends on how many of these qualities it possesses and to what degree. With this vocabulary, it possible to characterize the intrusiveness of alternative enforcement strategies with greater, but still rough, precision. To see how the vocabulary works, and to remind ourselves about the minimal degree of intrusiveness associated with our standard enforcement machinery, it is useful to review the machinery we use for enforcing laws against street offenses such as homicides, assaults, robberies, and rapes.

Enforcement Against Street Offenses

The standard enforcement procedures for street offenses can be

28

described quite simply. Typically, a uniformed, overt patrol roams the city watching for these offenses. While the reach of this patrol is fairly extensive, in the sense that it covers broad swaths of space and time, it is typically restricted to physical surveillance of public spaces and is focused on activities and places rather than persons. Moreover, the patrol is typically not very intensive: while its potential reach is large, its actual reach is quite limited. Of course, enforcement strategists may sometimes choose to give relatively greater attention to some piece of their terrain and thereby increase the intensiveness of surveillance in that area at the expense of intensiveness in the other areas for which they are responsible. But still, patrol operations are legally barred from invading private spaces and are traditionally reluctant to follow persons closely rather than observe spaces or activities. Finally, the patrol operations are overt and are not deceptive.

This relatively unobtrusive form of uniformed patrol is the only government information-gathering activity until an offense occurs. After a crime is committed and reported, a different form of government information gathering begins. It becomes more extensive in the sense that previous restrictions on government surveillance may now be breached, or the self-imposed boundaries expanded. Upon a showing of probable cause, the private spaces of suspects may be invaded. Homes can be searched and conversations monitored. Moreover, the surveillance may now be organized around persons rather than activities and places. The surveillance also becomes more intensive within the relatively narrow areas indicated by the investigation. Special efforts, including rewards, promises of future consideration, and so on, may be used to recruit co-conspirators as witnesses. Finally, some deception (and even instigation) may be used to identify and apprehend the offender. Thus, once an offense has occurred, government surveillance becomes much more intrusive with respect to all dimensions except one aspect of extensiveness; that is, the number of people, places, and activities that are vulnerable to government surveillance. The scope of these methods is tightly restricted by the limited number of people and activities relevant to the question of culpability for a specific known offense.

Note that a key concept structuring government information gathering for this type of offense is the concept of an investigative predicate.

The establishment of a predicate—some reason to believe that a crime has occurred in a specific area—stands between the limited, superficial (though wide) surveillance associated with overt patrol and the much more intrusive surveillance associated with investigation. The predicate justifies the intrusive surveillance by assuring people that a crime has been committed and thereby making it very likely that an enforcement benefit will result if more intrusive methods are allowed. It limits the intrusiveness of the methods by assuring that relatively intrusive forms of surveillance will be applied to only a small number of people, places, and activities. Thus, narrow investigative predicates assure a very favorable relationship between enforcement effectiveness and the intrusiveness of enforcement methods.

In enforcing against street offenses, then, we can maintain a satisfactory level of enforcement with minimal intrusive government surveillance. The effort to detect the offenses leaves much to private individuals and relies only on a minimally intrusive overt patrol effort. The more intrusive methods associated with investigation are unleashed only after an offense has been committed, and are narrowed and limited to the restricted number of people and activities plausibly connected to the known offense. Deception, recruitment of witnesses, and instigation are employed only rarely.

Enforcement Against Invisible Offenses

The enforcement problem changes dramatically when we turn to invisible offenses. For such offenses, enforcement must face the usual demanding investigative challenge of linking a known offense to a specific offender. But what is unusually problematic about invisible offenses is that enforcement faces an equally difficult task simply in detecting offenses. From the point of view of minimizing intrusiveness, equipping enforcement agencies to detect as well as investigate offenses will always create significant problems. Without a complaining victim or witness, we do not know where official surveillance should begin or end. Without a known offense, it is difficult to rely on predicates and the probable-cause standard to regulate degrees of intrusiveness. The problem, then, is that we might end up using enforcement methods whose degree of intrusiveness is characteristic of investigations, but using them for broad surveillance purposes spanning a large area of possible offenses and offenders. Detecting invisible offenses may require a higher degree of intrusion than we think appropriate. To explore the extent to which this is true, let us consider four enforcement techniques for detecting invisible offenses.

One is to increase the intensity of overt official patrols in areas where invisible offenses might occur. For victimless crimes such as narcotics and prostitution, this could take the form of denser patrolling in areas where such activities are common. For white-collar offenses such as employer and client fraud, overt patrol takes the form of audits of official records.[22] For political corruption, patrol becomes requirements of financial disclosure that allow easier detection of potential conflicts of interest.[23] For toxic wastes, overt patrol is managed by requirements that manufacturers report quantities of waste handled and disposed, and routine compliance audits of these records.[24]

Patrolling to discover extortionate crimes is probably the most difficult. One possibility is to interview people showing up at hospitals or doctors' offices with evidence of beating to determine if they are victims of loan sharks, spouses, offenders whose crimes they witnessed, and so on.[25] A way to patrol for cases of police brutality is routinely to photograph all arrested persons. Finally, patrolling for offenses such as drunk driving, speeding, illegal carrying of weapons, and so on can be accomplished through routine physical surveillance.

This brief review serves to show that opportunities to detect invisible offenses through overt patrol efforts do exist. They take different forms as one moves from one offense to another. Sometimes they rely on what we ordinarily think of as uniformed patrol. Other times they resemble audit and regulatory functions. What makes them similar is that they are all efforts to monitor, however superficially, relatively large areas within which specific offenses might occur without evidence that offenses have been committed. Moreover, they accomplish this overtly. There is no effort to disguise or conceal the monitoring effort, though there may be some uncertainty as to exactly when and where the surveillance will occur.

To describe the similar characteristics of these patrol efforts is also to describe their weaknesses. Because they are extensive, they are rarely intensive. It is simply too expensive to search broad areas thoroughly.

Moreover, because they are overt, offenders can arrange for their offenses to take place out of view. In short, these methods have the usual weaknesses of patrol functions: superficiality and visibility. They may require offenders to be cautious, and they may occasionally uncover an offense in progress, but one suspects that it is fairly easy for offenders to evade such operations. In this, overt patrol efforts are not dissimilar to ordinary patrol by uniformed officers in cars, commonly directed at street crime. We imagine that random motor patrols will observe offenses in progress, but the fact of the matter is that they rarely do.[26] The offenses are hidden until a citizen mobilizes the police, and even then, the mobilization usually comes too late to catch the offender.[27]

These observations suggest a second potential strategy in patrolling for invisible crimes: encouraging victims and witnesses to report the offenses, despite their hesitations. At a minimum, this involves reducing the hassle associated with reporting offenses. To this end, we remind people of the acts prohibited by law; give them a toll-free, 24-hour hotline to call; and accept tips from anonymous as well as identified complainants. Such strategies have been tried routinely in dealing with narcotics, illegal possession and transfer of weapons, and fraud in government programs.[28] Somewhat more ambitiously, we have sometimes *required* people in a position to witness offenses to report when they have done so. Thus, auditors are required to report on financial discrepancies, and physicians are required to report bullet wounds or possible instances of child and spouse abuse.[29] Even more ambitiously, we have tried to reassure victims and witnesses by providing them with protection and special kinds of service.[30] Such programs are particularly important in encouraging people to report on extortionate crimes such as loansharking, obstruction of justice, and police brutality. Finally, we often offer to pay people for information leading to the arrest and conviction of offenders. This, for example, is an important mode of enforcement against income tax evasion.[31] Private individuals are offered a share of whatever the government recovers as a reward for directing the Internal Revenue Service to people who may be cheating on their taxes.

Again, this quick review shows that some options exist for stimulating the flow of information from private citizens, even when dealing with invisible crimes. But to list the possibilities is also to reveal weaknesses.

32

We worry that the private surveillance stimulated by these strategies will be spotty and motivated by inappropriate private motives, and will generate false allegations. In effect, by leaving the burden of detection in private hands, and by making it convenient and even profitable for private individuals to make complaints, government surveillance ends up being directed by the whims and passions of private callers—a system of surveillance that may be no less intrusive and conceivably less fair than a system where the government assumes more of the burden of surveillance. (Of course, similar objections can be made against relying on private individuals to report street crimes such as robbery and assault. And, indeed, charges in such cases are often made or withheld by private individuals for reasons that have nothing to do with the legal question of whether an offense has been committed.) But for invisible offenses where the incentives of the victims and witnesses are weaker from the outset, the objections seem to acquire additional weight.

A third strategy in patrolling for invisible offenses is simply an extension of offering to pay people to report on offenses: namely, the recruitment of informants. After all, the only thing that distinguishes informants from paid "tipsters" is that informants have a continuing relationship with enforcement agencies. The continuing relationship is significant because it means that the informant loses the status of a private citizen and becomes, in an important sense, an employee or agent of the government. The informant acquires the interests of the government in observing the world, and loses the presumption of disinterest and innocence of other private citizens. Moreover, he or she operates deceptively; the relationship with the government is concealed from those the informant observes and deals with. Thus, informants can be thought of as covert government patrols reporting more or less regularly on a variety of possible offenses and offenders.[32]

It is useful to pause for a moment and consider the kind of social position informants would have to occupy to make a continuing relationship with an enforcement agency worthwhile. The simple answer is that they must be in a position to provide a *continuing* flow of information about criminal offenses: they may be in charge of records commonly used as evidence in criminal cases (for example, telephone records, bank records, travel records, and so on); they may engage in occupations that allow them to see the fruits of criminal activity (pawnbrokers, or tax accountants); they live or work in areas where criminal activity is planned or executed (a hotel clerk in an area of prostitution, a bartender in a nightclub frequented by criminals, or a police officer involved in processing prisoners); they may associate with frequent offenders (the gardener for an organized crime figure, or the childhood friend of a bank robber, or the uncle of a known narcotics dealer, for example); or they themselves may be criminal conspirators. The important fact to notice in this list is that many of the positions are valuable because they are linked to potential *offenders* rather than to knowledge of *offenses*. Recruiting informants by virtue of their association with offenders as distinguished from their relationship to criminal actions crosses an important line in terms of the intrusiveness of government surveillance. Yet it seems likely that this is an important basis for recruiting informants.

Informants can and do play an important role in uncovering invisible offenses. Their role in victimless crimes such as narcotics, gambling, and prostitution is well known.[33] They are also crucially involved in exposing criminal conspiracies that have not yet matured. In principle, they probably *could* be important in exposing white-collar crimes, political corruption, extortion, police brutality, and obstruction of justice. That they have not yet been extensively used in these areas is due less to their inadequacy than to current conventions. We have typically thought of informants as being drawn from the underworld. Consequently, it has seemed odd to think of recruiting informants from the ranks of business owners whose firms generate or dispose toxic wastes, or police officers in departments suspected of systematic civil rights violations, or politicians and public officials managing programs in which large amounts of money are at stake. Yet, there is no reason to suppose that informants could not be developed in these areas if we wanted to use them to enforce against white-collar crime, police brutality, or public corruption.

The strengths of informants in enforcing against invisible offenses are also their weaknesses. As deceptive government agents selected by virtue of their proximity to criminal offenders and offenses, they are in a position to see and hear a great deal. They will see many offenses that would otherwise be invisible. On the other hand, they will see a lot that is not unlawful. Unless their social position restricts their observations to

34

specific offenses and offenders (which makes them more like complaining witnesses for specific offenses than informants with continuing relationships to enforcement agencies), the range of activities and people that falls under their scrutiny is quite large. Moreover, in conducting their observations for the government, they easily cross important boundaries: intruding into private spaces, overhearing conversations, taking advantage of friendship, and so on. Thus, their surveillance is quite extensive. The intensiveness of their surveillance is determined by how many of them exist and how active they are on behalf of the government. It is worth noting in this regard that the economic arrangements between informants and the government allow the government to operate a large number at a relatively low cost, at least when compared to undercover agents. The reason is that while informants work full time for the government by being constantly aware of what is going on around them and having the government's interest in mind, they are paid only as part-time employees. Typically, they receive small, irregular payments as a retainer, and larger bonuses when they contribute information of unusual value. This arrangement is very favorable to the government. Finally, informants are always deceptive and occasionally are involved in instigating as well as simply observing. Thus, their value as instruments of government surveillance is matched (some would say over-matched) by their intrusiveness.

A fourth strategy that enforcement agencies can follow in ferreting out invisible offenses is to rely on undercover agents. To the extent that they are merely passive observers, undercover agents resemble informants, and a similar analysis of positioning and intrusiveness applies. The major difference between the two modes concern cost. To field undercover agents to conduct surveillance as informants do, the government must not only pay a full-time salary to agents in the field, but must also pay to establish the position of the agents (e.g., train them to be bartenders, assign them to cultivate a relationship, and so on). Thus, for any given level of expenditure, undercover agents will produce a level of surveillance that is less extensive and less intensive than could be produced by informants.[34]

The more common role for undercover agents, then, is not passive surveillance, but instigation. In order to shorten the amount of time and effort associated with a passive surveillance, the police arrange to have an offense take place while they are watching. We are apt to think of instigation as an investigative tool rather than a detection or patrol technique. Indeed, some have sought to limit the use of undercover operations to situations in which there is probable cause to believe that an offense has occurred or is imminent. The fact of the matter is, however, that instigation techniques can be and are used as patrol methods as well as investigative methods. For example, undercover agents sometimes set up fencing operations, trucking companies, or narcotics deals; wander into parks at night without knowing in advance who will show up to sell stolen goods or attack a vulnerable-looking person; suggest a sweetheart labor deal; or offer a kilo of heroin. Typically, some predicate rationalizing such operations exists, otherwise the expense of these operations, to say nothing of the intrusion, is hard to justify. But in many situations, the predicate is much broader and less specific than ordinarily required by the concept of probable cause.

Undercover operations can be and are very important in enforcing against victimless crimes and conspiracies. They could be important in areas such as extortion, political corruption, police brutality, criminal tax evasion, and toxic wastes. But again, their virtues as enforcement techniques are the liabilities in terms of intrusiveness. They are exceedingly intrusive in that they depend on deception and instigation. On the other hand, because of their cost, the government surveillance they generate is less extensive than that created by informants. Limiting the use of undercover operations to situations where probable cause could be established is certainly desirable, but if we established such a restriction, this technique would become useless as a way of detecting invisible offenses. Inasmuch as the main problem with invisible offenses is detecting them, this restriction on the use of undercover operations would cripple enforcement efforts against invisible offenses.

So far, we have been discussing techniques for detecting invisible offenses. Of necessity, this involves searching both extensively and intensively to locate the offenses, organizing the surveillance around offenders, using deception, motivating witnesses, and instigating offenses. That is, the strategies depend on inherently intrusive qualities. In this enterprise, indignant victims and witnesses are sorely missed. Overt patrols specially designed to be intensive in areas where invisible offenses are likely to occur fail to compensate fully for the loss of victims. Special efforts to mobilize victims and witnesses yield some response, but the response is likely to be thin and sporadic. Thus, the patrolling function turns inevitably to informants and undercover operations to help locate the offenses. Although such techniques are intrusive, there seems to be no other way to develop information about invisible offenses.

Because the patrol function depends heavily on informants and undercover operations, it is likely that the investigative function will depend fairly heavily on these techniques as well. In effect, informants and undercover operations tend to blur the distinction between detecting and investigating offenses: they happen almost simultaneously. Thus, the enforcement effort against invisible offenses is likely to be dominated by the most intrusive enforcement methods: informants and undercover operations spread rather broadly through the world.

The Challenge of Invisible Offenses

If it is true that invisible offenses require especially intrusive enforcement measures, then the existence of these offenses challenges the principles that have guided us in the selection of enforcement measures and confront us with painful choices. Specifically, our complacent assumptions about the balance between the principles of impartial enforcement of laws on one hand and the protection of privacy on the other become unsettled. We discover that one or the other principle must be honored less rigorously than we would like. Either we must accept inadequate enforcement against these offenses (thereby accepting the material losses associated with higher levels of these offenses as well as a breach in the principle of impartial enforcement of the laws), or we must accept a high degree of intrusiveness.

There is a further complication. Many of the techniques and methods that seem necessary in attacking invisible offenses are helpful in attacking street offenses. In fact, intensive overt patrols, special efforts to mobilize citizens, informants, and undercover operations are all now being used in efforts to control street crime. In fact, we are coming to realize that the level and quality of enforcement against street crime we received with the traditional methods of surveillance was much less than we had hoped. Some of the most serious crimes, such as robbery, assaults, homicides, and rapes, committed among strangers in public locations are not only not being prevented, but are also not being solved by traditional methods.[35] It is plausible that more proactive methods could be more successful.

Given these difficulties, we can choose to respond to the challenge of invisible offenses in one of three ways. We can decide that the offenses are not worth enforcing against and strike them from the books, or let them die of neglect. This has been the recommended solution for many victimless crimes. It has also been commonly recommended for the "crimes aborning" categories, such as conspiracies, possession of burglary tools, possession of guns, and so on. Perhaps this is wise. The case seems much harder, however, when the offenses to be dropped include extortion, obstruction of justice, police brutality, political corruption, illegal disposal of hazardous wastes, and criminal tax fraud.

If we decide that we cannot afford simply to ignore these offenses, we could make a second response. We could propose a principle of minimal intrusiveness consistent with effective enforcement against serious invisible offenses. This principle would not bar intrusive measures in all circumstances. Nor would it limit their use to situations where probable cause could be established. Instead, judgments would have to be made with respect to the various kinds of offenses in particular areas at particular times. The more serious the offense appeared, the more tolerable would intrusive measures become. This seems to be our current implicit policy.

A third more radical response would be to extend the principle of minimally intrusive measures to ordinary street crimes and effectively change our current conceptions about the organization of government surveillance. It would accept intensive patrols, special efforts to mobilize citizens, and use of informants and undercover operations as ordinary parts of our efforts to enforce existing laws against all crimes, rationally, effectively, and decently.

My own view is that we are not yet ready to respond to the challenge of invisible offenses and intrusive investigative techniques with any of these general policy lines. We simply have not thought enough about nor had enough documented experience with the intrusive enforce-

38

ment methods to understand what is at stake in using or failing to use them for some or all categories of offenses. We need to arrange for some common law to develop quickly in this area. To this end, we should allow—even encourage—enforcement agencies to experiment with some of the techniques directed at different sorts of offenses. At the same time, we should step up efforts to document that experience, to see what happens both in individual cases and in terms of aggregate performance. Finally, we should analyze that experience—trying to locate the important social values at stake in the use of these techniques—and the real nature of the links between the intrusive methods and the important social values.

One can imagine developing this body of knowledge through the courts, but it might be quicker and more effective to allow this development within the administrative agencies of the criminal justice system overseen by the courts. In effect, rather than imagine at the outset that all important issues in this area should or will be covered by constitutional principle, it might be better to think of invisible offenses and intrusive methods as primarily an administrative problem whose solution might have constitutional implications, and leave most of the burden of fact gathering and policy development to an administrative agency. To be consistent with the degree of responsibility entrusted to it, the administrative agency would have to represent broad social interests in civil liberties; in fair, rational, and effective enforcement; and in justice. Although no one quite believes that police agencies now represent this sort of institution, it might be possible to arrange oversight or review committees for police agencies that could review with them both existing policies regulating intrusive enforcement methods and their actual experience. Such arrangements might lead more quickly and more surely to the development of effective policies in these areas than reliance on the courts.

In sum, I think we should resist the urge to regulate the use of intrusive enforcement methods prematurely. I also think we should resist the temptation to rely on the courts as the major policy-making agency. Instead, we should allow some systematic experimentation with managing these methods so that we can find out what is really at stake, and base our policies on experience.

NOTES

1. The President's Commission on Law Enforcement and Administration of Justice, *The Challenge of Crime in a Free Society* (Washington, D.C.: U.S. Government Printing Office, 1967) pp. 7–12.

2. It is interesting to contrast our approach to police departments with, for example, our approach to a regulatory agency such as the Food and Drug Administration. The enormous body of Fourth Amendment law makes it seem as though all important questions concerning government information-gathering methods raise constitutional issues. Consequently, we have the Supreme Court examining police patrol strategies in microscopic detail. In the regulatory area, we assume state power is less directly engaged, and therefore that fewer constitutional issues arise. As a result, the agencies are left with more discretion to establish policies and procedures in accord with an administrative rationale emphasizing appropriate purposes, fair and economical procedures, and so on. Yet the consequences of regulatory action are often as significant as criminal enforcement activities. I sometimes wonder whether we would have as much Fourth Amendment law as we now have, and if it would be of the same character, if we had invented municipal police departments *after* we had invented the idea of administrative agencies rather than before.

3. In a forthcoming publication, my colleague, Professor Philip B. Heymann, illustrates the great latitude that constitutional principles leave in relying on undercover operations, grand jury investigations, and informants. See Philip B. Heymann, "From Hoffa to Abscam by Way of Koreagate: Thinking About Civil Liberties and Law Enforcement."

4. This is not a constitutional principle, but it has great power as a legal and political idea. Indeed, it is precisely this principle that (however modestly) limits the discretion of prosecutors. See James L. Vorenberg, "Decent Restraint of Prosecutional Power," 94 *Harv. L. Rev.* 7 (May, 1981). The crucial Supreme Court case allowing fair and rational prosecutorial decision is *Oyler* v. *Bates* (1961).

5. This principle provides an important part of the motivation for focusing attention on white-collar crime. See Mark H. Moore, "Notes Towards a National Strategy to Deal With White Collar Crime," in Herbert Edelhautz and Charles Rogovin, *A National Strategy for Containing White Collar Crime* (Lexington, Mass.: D.C. Heath and Company, 1980).

6. Perhaps the most important difference between the way lawyers think and the way policy analysts, managers, and economists think is that lawyers tend to think of lexically and hierarchically ordered values, while the others think of more fungible values where achievements with respect to one interest can be traded for losses on others. To a degree, this corresponds to making decisions on the basis of constitutional principles rather than administrative rationality. Part of the argument of this article is that we might usefully think of enforcement strategies as raising primarily administrative and policy rather than constitutional issues.

7. For empirical studies of the extent to which we depend on private citizens for identifying and apprehending offenders, see Peter W. Greenwood, et al., *The Criminal Investigation Process* (Lexington, Mass.: D.C. Heath and Co., 1977).

8. The most important legal doctrine here is the need for warrants to make arrests and searches. This constitutional requirement—paired with current strategies of policing—assures that most enforcement activity will occur after an offense has occurred.

9. The extent to which citizens control enforcement activities by triggering their response is rarely appreciated. In effect, anyone with a dime can command some degree of police attention. This suggests a high degree of democratic control over police operations. On the other hand, the police may not patrol all parts of a city with equal interest, and they may not give equal attention to all complaints. For a discussion of systematic social biases in policing, see Donald Black, *The Manners and Customs of Policing* (New York: Academic Press, 1980).

10. Edwin M. Schur, *Crimes Without Victims* (Englewood, N.J.: Prentice-Hall, 1965).

11. James Q. Wilson, *The Investigators* (New York: Basic Books, 1978).

12. Herbert Packer, *The Limits of the Criminal Sanction* (Stanford, Calif.: Stanford University Press, 1968).

13. I am indebted to Professor Heymann for this point.

14. The original court interpretations of the Fourth Amendment's guarantee of the "right of the people to be secure in their persons, houses, papers and effects, against unreasonable searches and seizures" emphasized a property concept that gave special status to dwelling places. More recently, the Court has relied on a more abstract notion of a privacy interest as the basis of the Fourth Amendment protections. The change occurred with *Katz* v. *U.S.,* 389 U.S. 347 (1967). Still, dwelling places retain a special status and they are protected against warrantless searches more determinedly than other locations. See *Coolidge* v. *N.H.,* 403 U.S. 443 (1971).

15. One of the most surprising exceptions to the Court's steadfast commitment to protecting "reasonable expectations of privacy" is its willingness to allow testimony from a suspect's close friend who also happens to be an informant. See *Hoffa* v. *U.S.,* 385 U.S. 206 (1966). This contrasts oddly with the Court's protection of professional relationships such as doctor-patient.

16. This standard was set out in *Katz*.

17. I am indebted to Professor Heymann for emphasizing this point. For an extensive discussion of privacy interests, see Ruth Gavison, "Privacy and the Limits of Law," 89 *Yale L.J.* 3 (January 1980): 421–471.

18. For further elaboration of this point, see Sanford Levinson's chapter, "Infiltration and Betrayal: A Legal and Theoretical Analysis," in this volume.

19. Again, I am indebted to Professor Heymann for emphasizing this point.

20. Wilson, *The Investigators.*

21. Economists tend to view great benefits and temptations as analytically similar to great penalties and threats. Both motivate behavior by changing a person's calculus about the consequences of given actions. Thus, instigation can be coercive by making offenses very tempting to offenders. Even if one thinks that this way of thinking distorts the meaning of "coercive," it is interesting to note that the law also tends to treat both threats and temptations symmetrically: their presence in a situation makes it more difficult to understand the true motivations and values of the offenders. Since one must have an improper mental state to be judged guilty of most offenses, the confusion introduced by unusual threats and temptations makes it more problematic to find an offender guilty of a crime.

22. Mark H. Moore "Notes Towards a National Strategy to Deal with White Collar Crime."

23. For illustrative statutes, see Massachusetts State Ethics Commission, General Laws of the Commonwealth of Massachusetts, Ch. 268B, section 2.

24. Melvin T. Axilband and Herbert Edelhartz, "An Introduction to Hazardous Waste for Prosecutors and Investigators," mimeo. (Seattle, Washington: Batille Research Institute, undated).

25. For an analysis of strategies to deal with extortion, see Jay Francis, "Enforcement of Extortion Laws in Boston," unpublished mimeo. (Cambridge, Mass.: Kennedy School of Government, Harvard University, 1978).

26. George L. Kelling, et. al, *The Kansas City Preventive Patrol Experiment* (Washington, D.C.: Police Foundation, 1974).

27. William G. Spelman, *Calling the Police: A Replication of the Citizen Reporting Component of the Kansas City Response Time Analysis* (Washington, D.C.: Police Executive Research Forum, 1981).

28. For several years, a "heroin hotline" was maintained by the U.S. Customs Service to catch smugglers at the border. Similarly, the Bureau of Alcohol, Tobacco and Firearms has mounted a public campaign to "Disarm the Criminal" complete with posters describing the legal requirements of the Gun Control Act, and giving a number to call for tips. Finally, government "whistleblowers" have been encouraged through various protections to give information about "fraud, waste and abuse" to inspectors-general.

29. M.H. Alderman, *Child Abuse and Neglect Reporting Laws* (Washington, D.C.: Herner & Co., 1979).

30. The most common are victims/witnesses services operated as adjuncts to courts. For an evaluation of their impact, see Vera Institute of Justice, "Impact Evaluation of the Victim/Witness Assistance Project's Appearance Management Activities," mimeo. (New York: Vera Institute of Justice, 1976). More ambitious is the federal government's Witness Protection Program managed by the United States Marshals. This program offers to relocate key witnesses and equip them with new identities.

31. That this tactic remains an important enforcement practice in IRS was confirmed by several high level Internal Revenue Service officials attending an executive training program at the Kennedy School of Government in the summer of 1982.

32. Michael R. Bromwich, "The Use and Control of Informants," mimeo. (Cambridge, Mass.: Kennedy School of Government, Harvard University, 1980).

33. Malachi Harney and John C. Cross, *The Informer in Law Enforcement* (Springfield, Illinois: Charles C Thomas, 1960). See also Mark H. Moore, *Buy and Bust: The Effective Regulation of an Illicit Market in Heroin* (Lexington, Mass.: D.C. Heath and Co., 1977), and Wilson, *The Investigators.*

34. Brenda Gruss, "The Detection and Investigation of Crime By Citizens, Informants, Undercover Agents, and Undercover Operations: A Comparative Perspective," mimeo. (Cambridge, Mass.: Kennedy School of Government, Harvard University, 1981).

35. Clearance rates for robbery are currently less than 20 percent. See Greenwood, et al., *The Criminal Investigative Process.*

3

Under Cover: The Hidden Costs of Infiltration

Sanford Levinson*

CONSIDER THE MOVIE *The Sting.* In that lighthearted film, Paul Newman and Robert Redford (or, rather, the characters they acted) devised a
"Big Con," outwitting the gambler played by Robert Shaw. They created an entire reality—a Chicago betting parlor—for Shaw's observation, even if not for his benefit. As viewers we took delight in knowing
what Shaw did not—that nothing was as it appeared to be, and that he

* Reprinted with permission from *The Hastings Center Report,* August 1982, pp. 29-37.

was about to pay a big price for his faith in what Erving Goffman has helped us to recognize as "normal appearances."[1]

Now think of the well-known social science experiments carried out by Stanley Milgram. Two people come to a psychology laboratory—one is designated a "teacher" and the other a "learner." The experimenter explains that the research is concerned with the effects of punishment on learning. The "teacher" believes that he is inflicting ever-increasing electric shocks on the "learner," when he responds incorrectly to questioning. But the "learner" is not just another subject, but an actor, who receives no shock at all yet protests his pain vehemently to the naive subject/"teacher." This kind of con game has been justified as leading to important knowledge about the psychology of obedience.[2]

Finally, consider this familiar scene, which was replayed frequently on television screens. A white-robed "sheik" sits in a hotel room talking to a parade of elected officials, describing his problem in obtaining legal entry into the United States and offering cash in return for help. His story elicits boastful promises and eager offers of assistance. The "sheik," of course, was no Arab but an FBI undercover agent. The ABSCAM operation is yet another example of a con game, this one justified by its potential to expose corrupt public servants.

Yet what if Newman and Redford had gained their revenge by beating up their victim instead of outwitting him? Or, what if the "learner" in Milgram's experiment had actually received the purported electric shocks, so that at least one importantly deceptive aspect of the experiment had become altogether genuine? And, finally, what if the "sheik" had kidnapped one of the official's children (or even pets) in an effort to see if the ransom might include betrayal of public confidence?

Presumably we would feel differently about these revised situations, though it is worthwhile to ask why. Is physical violence necessarily more objectionable than the use of deceit to attain the same end? Sissela Bok thinks not:

> Deceit and violence—these are the two forms of deliberate assault on human beings. Both can coerce people into acting against their will. Most harm that can befall victims through violence can come to them also through deceit. But deceit controls more subtly, for it works on belief as well as action.

44

Even Othello, whom few would have dared to subdue by force, could be brought to destroy himself and Desdemona through falsehood.[3]

Iago, the source of Othello's downfall, has become a central literary incarnation of malignity, motiveless or otherwise. Society's acceptance of the con game—and willingness on occasion even to identify with the con artist—depends partly on dehumanizing the victim and being willing to ignore the implications of legitimating the con. Yet in all con games—no matter what the context—both victim and con artist are diminished by the encounter. And in the case of the undercover agent, the example I will develop more fully later, we lack both an ethical norm and a public policy that takes account of the damage done to the agent, the victim, and society. We have neglected to examine the legal and ethical implications of allowing infiltrators to enter the private lives of others, ultimately to betray their trust.

Public Selves and Private Selves

The essence of the con is that the victim's perception does not fit the underlying reality, which is known only to the manager of the con. Things may be rearranged so that they appear to be something that they are not—forged documents, fake jewelry, phony residences, for example. More important, in most con games people misrepresent themselves; they pretend to be criminals, political sympathizers, doctors, or friends, when they are not. Our ability to distinguish the con artist's false identity from the "real" one rests ironically on our knowledge of our own multiple selves. We could not recognize, accept, and even admire the illusion of the con if we did not relate the multiple identities to our sense of ourselves as both public selves (the face we present to the world) and private selves (the one that we show only to a few).

A poignant recognition of the difference between public and private selves is given in Chekov's description of the principal character in "Lady with the Little Dog":

> Judging others by himself, he did not believe what he saw, and always fancied that every man led his real, most interesting life under cover of secrecy as under cover of night. The personal life of every individual is based on secrecy, and perhaps it is

partly for that reason that civilized man is so nervously anxious that personal privacy should be so respected.[4]

Charles Fried builds on a similar recognition in his influential analysis of privacy, which is related to the possibility of love and friendship. What distinguishes these exquisite relationships from mundane life is intimacy. Fried says,

> To be friends or lovers persons must be intimate to some degree with each other. Intimacy is the sharing of information about one's actions, beliefs or emotions which one does not share with all, and which one has the right not to share with anyone. By conferring this right, privacy creates moral capital which we spend on friendship and love.[5]

We generally smile at two lovers sharing their secrets. But if we fear that those "actions, beliefs or emotions" that are unknown to us might in fact be turned against us, then we must come to grips with what I call the paranoid underside of liberal political thought, that theoretical tradition that has been at greatest pains to separate private persona (and space) from public socialization (and scrutiny).[6]

In the social image described (if not endorsed) by classical liberalism, atomistic individuals seek to maximize their own interests. In the absence of settled authority (backed by public power), each individual has cause to feel afraid of enough other people so that he or she becomes insecure about life, liberty, or property. Moreover, as Thomas Hobbes pointed out so cogently, "The nature of war, consisteth not in actual fighting; but in the known disposition thereto; during all the time there is not assurance to the contrary."[7] The "known disposition" is ruthless self-interest. Even peaceful behavior, Hobbes says, cannot be trusted because it might be designed precisely to lull you into sleep, when your sheep-appearing neighbor would reveal the wolf-like disposition to devour you. In such a world, Jean Bethke Elshtain declares, "The relations of Hobbesian beings to one another are guided by an instrumentalism shorn of sentiment."[8]

The liberal state—particularly as we in America tend to see it refracted through Hobbes or Locke, not to mention Rawls or Nozick—accepts this view of human nature as intractable and tries to create a set of institutional arrangements that will control the more predatory aspects of its citizens.[9] Terms like "friendship," "love," and "intimacy" are foreign to liberal politics, which has no coherent notion of community ("fraternity") or even of "public interest." Yet most liberals seem to believe that friendship and love are possible in the nonpolitical realm. Indeed, the argument runs, the social stability provided by the liberal state makes possible the creation of rich private lives.

But why should our private psychologies and our public ones be so different? If we are capable of achieving true intimacy in a private relationship, why can we not achieve at least some measure of intimacy as members of a common society? If we cannot do so because of the limits of our egocentricity, then why do we think that these limits will be overcome simply by trusting fewer individuals? If we do not trust our impressions of strangers because we fear their secret selves, why do we put greater trust in our impressions of those to whom we are closest? May they not betray us by revealing our secret selves to our enemies? (And, of course, might it not be the case that our secret life is in fact devoted to harming those enemies who thus quite justifiably fear us and desire knowledge of our secrets?)

This paranoid view has led liberal society to perceive a need to infiltrate the private lives of those who might be secretly plotting its destruction, and it has justified the deceptions of those who are enlisted as infiltrators. A popular television series of the 1950s—Herb Philbrick's *I Led Three Lives*—had two morals: people who appeared trustworthy might in fact be Communists, therefore the essence of evil; and it was perfectly proper to attempt to uncover duplicity by employing duplicity oneself.[10] Such a view, though oversimple, is widely held today.

Yet most analyses of informing consider quite different kinds of behavior under the same rubric. Our moral assessment of undercover work may well depend on what kind of informing we mean. To explain, let me present three different views of the archetypal informer—Judas.

A Typology of Informers

In the Gospels, it is written that Judas, for no clear reason, decided to betray Christ and arranged to receive a payment upon his identifying Christ to the Roman authorities. Thereafter, at the Last Supper, he denied that he intended to betray Jesus, though he did so intend, as his subsequent behavior proved.

I am interested in examining not the psychology of Judas but the relationship between Christ and Judas and how that relationship would be affected depending on the type of informer Judas was. I also ignore the problem presented by Christ's presumed knowledge of the identity of his betrayer, although this problem presents the most exquisite difficulties in answering the question: was Christ or Judas the more truly deceived in their relationship?

The informer as snitch. Let us assume first that Judas turned Christ over the authorities immediately after his initial decision to betray him; there would have been no Last Supper. In this instance a person changed his mind about the duties he owed to another person and acted thereafter to "betray" that person. But there is no ground for believing that Judas would ever have presented himself falsely to Christ. That is, all their exchanges prior to the act of betrayal had been ones of authentic friendship and discipleship.

It is unrealistic to expect that one's friends will never change their minds about a relationship, that none of them will ever commit what might be perceived as an act of betrayal. As Michael Walzer has pointed out, the very esssence of life in a pluralistic society involves recognition of the extent to which our relationships are all contingent. "[A] pluralist," says Walzer, "is a man with more than one commitment, who may at any moment have to choose among his different obligations."[11] One might expect that the final act of friendship would be the informer's candid revelation as to his actions and the reasons for them. The person informed against will realize, of course, that he or she has, to use Fried's terminology, invested the moral capital of secrets poorly; but, as we shall see, still worse discoveries are possible.

To summarize: in this version, Judas acted in "good faith" toward Christ when receiving his secrets. Because he chose to reveal these secrets to the Roman authorities does not by itself mean that he deceived Christ. There is an all-important distinction between the informer as "snitch" and the undercover agent.

One more complication, to be examined more fully below, is the difference between Judas as a genuinely voluntary witness and his role as a *compelled* witness. What if, for example, the Roman authorities subpoenaed him to testify, on pain of punishment for failure to give testimony? Here the focus is not so much on what Judas ought to do as on the state that asks for such disclosure from intimates of the "target" who is the focus of suspicion. No analysis of privacy and its protections can avoid confronting the problem of testimonial privileges.

The informer as double-self. Contrast this notion of the Christ-Judas relationship with one in which the authorities said, "We need more evidence against Jesus. Return to him and engage him in a conversation about his mission. Try to get some solidly incriminating statements out of him to which you can testify." Judas would have returned and carried out his task. He would *now* in fact be presenting himself to Jesus as other than what he had become, that is, an agent of the state in opposition to Jesus. Judas would have had to deceive, which was not the case under the first model. He would have had to engage in a con game (as the Gospels suggest that to some extent he did).

Judas would have had to assume the role of a double-self, as secret agent. The head that was nodding no and the lips that were saying, "Not I, surely?" in answer to Christ's assertion that one of his disciples was to betray him were also linked to consciousness that was perhaps thinking, "This is just the evidence they need; perhaps they'll give me sixty pieces of silver." Judas may have thought, in this scenario, "He has not yet said anything of interest to the authorities; perhaps I should try to steer the conversation toward the subjects I know they are curious about."

The poignancy of the situation here, in part, comes from Judas's initial faithfulness as a disciple. There was once a genuine relationship between Judas and Jesus. Indeed, Judas was admitted to the Last Supper (and only he and Christ could have known that it was indeed to be the "Last Supper") because of this prior friendship. The betrayal suffered by Christ in this version is of a wholly different magnitude than that described in the first telling. And the scent of evil now emanates from Judas in a way that was not present in the first instance.

How much of the stench is connected with Judas's role as an agent of the state? Would we feel just as troubled if, for example, he had done his work for the Jerusalem *Times,* a local newspaper interested in exposing the truth about this cult figure Jesus, rumored not only to be a social revolutionary but even to have said something so contrary to ordinary decency as, "If any *man* come to me, and hate not his father, and mother, and wife, and children, and brethren, and sisters, yea, and his own life also, he cannot be my disciple."[12] To the extent that our attitude toward infiltration and deception varies according to the degree to which the state per se is involved, then we must ask ourselves to explain the basis for this presumed distinction.

The informer as wholly false self. In the second model of Judas, he had been at least at one point a genuine disciple. But what if that had never been the case? What if the authorities had suspected that Jesus was a subversive who needed to be investigated and had hired Judas to insinuate himself into Christ's retinue to observe him and gather evidence that might confirm their suspicions? The same disjunction between public and secret selves would have occurred, but the relationship would have been unauthentic from the very beginning. In both of the first two versions, Jesus is entitled to look on Judas as a disciple who betrayed him. But in this last example Judas was *never* a genuine disciple; he was only pretending to be one. Actors and actresses clue us in to their assumption of special selves by climbing on stages, dimming lights, and otherwise informing us that we are to join them in a common game of "let's pretend" (also known as the willing suspension of disbelief). What distinguishes a con game from a play is the absence of a common game.[13]

The Informer as a Social Subversive

What are the implications of adopting as a social policy the use of one or another of the three types of informers? The first type presents no very great ethical or legal problem so long as we assume that the decision to betray is voluntary in some reasonably strong sense. We might have qualms about the state's putting too much pressure on a person to turn in or testify against a former associate, but I find it almost impossible to argue that the state should ever protect A's secrets by preventing B's voluntary disclosure of them.

The second and third categories of informer, dealing with the conscious use by the state (or other institutions) of double-selves, is deeply subversive of the possibility of friendship, love, and trust. This use is

50

morally equivalent to the decision to use violence; indeed it is a kind of torture. Perhaps it can be defended, just as nonpacifists recognize the appropriate occasions for directed violence, but we should place greater barriers, including legal ones, in the way of casually embarking on such use.

As Goffman points out, our security about our lives is radically dependent on being able to trust "normal appearances," and attacks on this ability to trust may be devastating. For example, a woman is walking along a street at dusk and hears footsteps. She looks around and sees a priest, clutching his rosary. She relaxes, perhaps even slows down a bit in order to become part of his territorial space, in order to share the deference accorded priests. The priest, however, turns out to be a "priest," who pushes her into the bushes and mugs her. A mugging "priest" would create far more social disorder than a comparable spate of muggings by persons who fit our more common stereotypes of muggers, for our notion of what constitutes trustworthy appearances would be demolished. If a "mugging cop" joined a "mugging priest," then society would be disordered far more than by the depredations of criminals who have the courtesy to fit our preconceptions of the way they should look. Disguises may be more threatening than guns; at the very least, the artful disguise may draw from us what would otherwise be given only at the point of a gun.

Although the example involves a crime of violence, the thief could just as easily be in pursuit of information rather than tangible goods; the "mugging" need involve nothing more (or less) than the insinuation into one's allegedly private sphere of life for the purpose of gaining such information. Here, indeed, disguises may be even more effective than a gun, for one may reveal oneself more quickly and completely to a presumed friend or lover than to an obvious enemy, even an enemy brandishing a gun. The very rationale for the use of undercover agents comes from a recognition of the utility of invading private space in order to get valuable information.

Even as they play their roles, often with consummate skill, the more sensitive undercover agents nonetheless recognize the charged nature of their activities. Consider, for example, Lieutenant Joe Delaney of the Bergen County, New Jersey, Narcotics Task Force, who spent eleven months as "an Underworld Spy" following an attempt to bribe him.[14] At the behest of his superiors, to whom he reported the offer, Delaney began "posing as a crooked policeman" in an attempt to "infiltrate the underworld." He was remarkably successful; not the least measure of his success was his ability to record "devastating" statements on hidden electronic listening devices that he wore strapped to his body. As a result of evidence obtained through his infiltration, several members of New Jersey's organized crime network went to jail.

Delaney, however, had profoundly mixed feelings:

> . . . Lieutenant Delaney seems troubled by what he openly discusses as a "strange, odd" feeling that he has "betrayed" his victims on a personal level . . .
>
> "I was playing the part of their friend; talking to their wives and kids. . . ."
>
> Part of his unease, he agrees, rests on an aversion to snitching ingrained in his childhood in Chelsea and part is traceable, he suggests, to the sentimentality deriving from his Irish heritage.[15] But basically, he seems bothered by the damage the indictments have caused the "humanistic, the human part" of the people caught by his subterfuge.

Delaney's sense of disquiet may arise from his actions as a third-category, wholly false self. His concern manifests the reality of Peter Berger's comment: "If there is one universal, indeed, primeval principle of morality, it is that one must not deliver one's friends to their enemies."[16] Even if Berger's statement is overly simplistic in its own way, it helps to explain the disquiet felt by a genuinely courageous and public-spirited police officer like Lieutenant Delaney. Presumably he would have felt even worse had he been a type-II informer and therefore more genuinely a betrayer of his friends.

Infiltration and the Constitution

Delaney's tour as an underworld spy occurred wholly without judicial supervision. The decision to have him pose as a rogue cop and, ultimately, infiltrate even the family dinners of his victims was made by officials of the Bergen County police department. Although "official investigatory action that impinges on privacy must typically, in order to be constitutionally permissible, be subjected to the warrant requirement"

52

of the Fourth Amendment,[17] this is not the case when impingement involves the infiltration of private space by an undercover agent seeking only information (and incriminating statements) rather than tangible evidence (such as documents relating to loan-sharking).[18]

Indeed, the absence of a warrant requirement is only half the story, for the Fourth Amendment can be read as setting out a minimum requirement that even warrantless searches be "reasonable" with the opposite being also true: that "unreasonable" searches are illegal. Yet the courts have been no more willing to impose even a general requirement of reasonableness than a full-scale one for warrants.[19] Had the Bergen County police sought verbal information by listening in on telephone conversations, a warrant would have been required, setting out the probable cause to believe that wiretapping would result in the capture of relevant information. Not even "reasonableness" was formally required, however, before Lieutenant Delaney was sent on his way (though it was surely present, as was, in all likelihood, the probable cause necessary for a warrant). Why is this so?

To begin, note Justice Brennan's extremely influential dissenting opinion in *Lopez* v. *United States*. That case involved a federal agent who was recording his victim's statements on a pocket tape recorder. Although Brennan dissented from the majority's approval of submission of the taped evidence at trial, his analysis emphasized a distinction that has plagued subsequent discussion:

> There is a qualitative difference between electronic surveillance, whether the agents conceal the devices on their persons or in walls or under beds, and conventional police strategems such as eavesdropping and disguise. *The latter do not so seriously intrude upon the right of privacy. The risk of being overheard by an eavesdropper or betrayed by an informer or deceived as to the identity of one with whom one deals is probably inherent in the conditions of human society. It is the kind of risk we necessarily assume whenever we speak.* But as soon as electronic surveillance comes into play, the risk changes crucially. There is no security from that kind of eavesdropping, no way of mitigating the risk, and so not even a residuum of true privacy.[20]

Justice Brennan presents no cogent rationale for his casual acceptance of the use of disguise and deception by the police. Perhaps he thought that judicial toleration of such warrantless practice was too ingrained to be successfully challenged, so he chose to mount his attack on the basis of the "qualitative difference" between personal disguise and electronic surveillance. I certainly do not wish to challenge his animosity toward such surveillance, nor do I even wish to argue that there is no qualitative difference at all. But Justice Brennan's analysis has focused attention almost exclusively on the presence or absence of electronic invasion. However important that might be, it simply is not a tenable basis for the legal or ethical differentiation that his analysis has created.

Justice Brennan's words were quoted in perhaps the most important Supreme Court opinion yet written about "unwired" informers, *Hoffa v. United States*.[21] There the Court upheld the admission into evidence of the testimony of Edward Partin, a Teamsters Union official who, while acting as an informer for the Justice Department, ingratiated himself into Hoffa's entourage during an important trial involving the then-Teamster president in Nashville, Tennessee. The majority opinion emphasized that Hoffa welcomed Partin into his hotel suite. "Partin did not enter the suite by force or by stealth,"[22] unless one defines "stealth" as the nondisclosure of his informer status, a definition that would effectively bring to an end the freedom to use undercover agents without judicial supervision. Of course Partin was welcomed because Hoffa perceived him as a previously trusted associate, that is, a type-II informer. Justice Stewart, for the majority, wrote confidently that the Court had unanimously rejected any contention "that the Fourth Amendment protects a wrongdoer's misplaced belief that a person to whom he voluntarily confides his wrongdoing will not reveal it,"[23] with Brennan's *Lopez* dissent offered as evidence of the unanimity of the Court on this basic proposition.

Decided that same day was *Lewis v. United States*,[24] a case in which a federal undercover agent, a stranger to the convicted Lewis, pretended to be an ordinary drug buyer. As a result he was invited into Lewis's home, where a sale took place. Unlike *Hoffa*, there was no prior relationship between the undercover agent and the victim of the deception. In a brief opinion written by Chief Justice Warren, who had dissented in *Hoffa*, the Court upheld Lewis's conviction. "[I]n the detection of many types of crime, the Government is entitled to use decoys and to conceal the identity of its agents."[25] Here the type-III undercover agent made no

54

profession of "friendship," unlike *Hoffa,* and Lewis invited him into his home to conduct a straight business transaction. Warren was absolutely correct that, "were we to hold the deceptions of the agent in this case constitutionally prohibited, we would come near to a rule that the use of undercover agents in any manner is virtually unconstitutional per se";[26] he (and the Court) was unwilling to declare such a rule.

Even analysts generally critical of the latitude given undercover agents appear to agree with the result in *Lewis.* "[N]o 'reasonable' expectation of privacy can be grounded on an implicit or explicit representation by a stranger that he is indeed a criminal. To permit such deceptions will, after all, expose to police spying only those people who express to strangers a willingness to engage in criminal activity."[27] This rationale is persuasive, though, only if two conditions are met: first, we all agree on what counts as (properly) criminal conduct; and second, the undercover agent learns nothing more about a person than his or her willingness to *continue* violating the law. The first condition raises the question of so-called political crimes; the second, of entrapment or the generation of crimes that might otherwise go uncommitted.

Although the Court has continued to debate the role of the Fourth Amendment regarding electronic surveillance,[28] Justice Brennan's misguided comment in his *Lopez* dissent has apparently become accepted doctrine. Neither warrant nor even reasonableness seems necessary prior to a decision by a police department to attempt the infiltration of the life of a suspected criminal.[29]

Some particularly bothersome cases involving undercover agents have been handled under the doctrinal rubric of entrapment. However, entrapment, as currently interpreted by the Supreme Court, refers almost wholly to the subjective predisposition of a person to commit the crime in question. One reason for objecting to undercover agents is, to be sure, a fear that they will encourage the commission of offenses by persons who would otherwise remain law-abiding, but this fear is almost completely absent in cases like *Hoffa, Lewis,* or Lieutenant Delaney's. If one objects to certain kinds of undercover agents in those cases, the basis must be something other than fear of the dangers associated with entrapment. That basis could only be the importance of nondeceptive personal relationships themselves, which is precisely what is undercut by Justice Brennan's analysis.

Part of the problem with the Brennan analysis, and its subsequent unthinking repetition by the Court's majority, is its lack of differentiation among types of informers. It is not that Brennan's argument is wholly false; it is, rather, that he lumps together all types of informers.

Return to the first Judas, who repudiates his former loyalties to Jesus. I agree with Brennan that it is indeed "inherent in the conditions of human society" that we can never absolutely rely on even our most intimate associates to remain loyal to us. Such reliance would deny the very complexities of plural loyalties about which Walzer writes so eloquently. Furthermore, legal protections of A's expectations of privacy necessarily impinge on B's own autonomous choice to define him- or herself in terms other than as A's confidante. Indeed, one reason we are at risk even when we disclose ourselves to intimates is that it violates their own status as free human beings to *prevent* them from betraying us. They, like we, after all, might choose the demands of citizenship over those of friendship should we reveal ourselves to be antisocial.

I thus agree with the Supreme Court's recent decision in *Trammel* v. *United States*,[30] which abolished an aspect of the traditional marital privilege insofar as it allowed a defendant spouse to block adverse testimony of the other spouse even if offered voluntarily. The witness spouse still has the privilege to refuse to testify adversely, but it is now up to him or her whether or not to exercise it.

There is one acceptable rationale for testimonial privileges to be controlled by the one who confided the information: we want to encourage certain relationships—such as those of lawyer-client, and doctor-patient—that require discussion of intimate subjects even in the absence of intimacy. In such instances it probably makes sense not to recognize the autonomy of the lawyer, doctor, or social worker who is testifying, since he or she may have no genuine bonds of loyalty to inhibit disclosure of the dreadful secret. But this utilitarian rationale seems unavailable in regard to marriage, where the concern is intimacy itself. When the voluntary desire to protect the other is gone, so is the relationship.

Moreover, American law generally is unconcerned with protecting intimate relationships from the intrusive claims of the state for evidence.

56

Think of sixteen-year-old Kim Marshall, called to testify against her mother before a Las Vegas grand jury. Refusing to testify, she cited the biblical injunction to "honor thy father and mother."[31] At the time, the Justice Department was considering citing Ms. Marshall for contempt, though no such citation was filed.

How can one consistently exhibit outrage against infiltrating private lives while at the same time supporting the compelled testimony of friends, lovers, family members, and colleagues against those whom they would otherwise wish to protect by remaining silent? One reason for not simply relying on such compelled testimony, of course, is the tendency toward convenient forgetfulness on the part of such witnesses; undercover agents unburdened by personal loyalties are presumably more reliable, but the very willingness to call the lover or friend exhibits less than overwhelming regard for the relational values often commended by those who attack the use of secret agents.

My concern is principally for the person called upon to testify—the involuntary Judas, as it were; I have no great interest in protecting the victims of voluntary, type I Judases. Such "betrayals," after all, represent genuine crises of identity rather than the *denouement* of the act of posturing that is necessarily linked to the notion of undercover infiltration. The autonomous decisions of those associates who presented themselves to us in good faith are different from the kinds of decisions made by infiltrators.

"A person has an interest," George Dix has argued, "in knowing all relevant characteristics of those with whom he forms any personal relationships and of those to whom he discloses information concerning relationships with others."[32] Yet obviously we usually do not cross-examine individuals before we decide to begin treating them as (potential) friends; it is equally obvious that we are often disappointed in our initial assessments of people and end up withdrawing offers of friendship upon discovery of "relevant characteristics." It is not so much that we need to know all about those with whom we consider intimacy; indeed, it is unlikely that they would tell us "all" unless we were simultaneously investing some of our own Friedian capital of personal secrets. Instead we need to assume a certain level of good faith as being present in the encounter. We are not entitled to assume that strangers will turn out to

57

match our idealized expectations; but we are entitled to the belief that persons who present themselves to us will not actively be wishing us ill and using the encounter as a means of furthering their malevolence toward us.

This latter assumption of good faith (or at least of "non-bad faith") is undermined by the use of infiltrators. This assumption is as easily violated by "private" parties as by the state, one of the central perpetrators being the press. Thus newspaper reporters, in an effort to ferret out important information, have masqueraded as assembly-line workers, naive consumers, and bartenders.[33] Only a narrow lawyer can be happy with an argument that this kind of activity is protected by the First Amendment whereas police undercover work should be controlled by the Fourth Amendment. The nonlawyer will instantly ask what, besides the alleged commands of positive law, commends such a distinction. One reply is that the power of the state is special; to the extent that ours is a genuinely pluralistic society, however, the dilemma posed by undercover infiltrators cannot be made wholly synonymous with the particular problems posed by secret police.

Infiltration, whether by police or private citizen, would be impossible if society did not generally endorse the values (and possibility) of trust and intimacy. Although I suspect that the reaction of a Vietnam Veteran Against the War whose "best friend" turned out to be an informer—"I still don't trust a whole lot of people . . . I keep much more to myself than I did before the trial"[34]—is typical, the successful infiltrator depends on the nonparanoia of the victim. Even hardened Mafiosi turn out to be remarkably trusting.

There is, then, an essential dichotomy built into any society that regularly depends on infiltration for crime control, at least so long as the society also professes to value a private realm of trust and intimacy. To the extent that the public becomes more and more aware that people are not at all whom they appear to be, the trust necessary for successful infiltration will be harder to evoke (or more extreme "markers" of trustworthiness will be required, ranging from sexual intercourse to participation in illegal or otherwise socially stigmatic activity). One may lament this, of course, not only because it would make crime control

58

more difficult, but also because of the much more important damage to society itself.

The Law of Evidence as a Seamless Web

It is tempting to conclude by endorsing calls for more vigorous restraint on the use of police undercover agents by interpreting the Fourth Amendment to require a search warrant before placing agents in a context in which the effectiveness of an investigation depends on deceiving others. I do in fact support such restraint, of course, but it increasingly strikes me as too facile to conclude the discussion at this point. Whatever the benefits to lawyers of thinking in terms of isolated Fourth Amendment values and rights, public debate must be informed by a more holistic understanding. The Fourth Amendment is part of a wider structure of constitutional values, and it is possible that the failure to protect privacy more adequately is a response to defects in the more general structure. Thus my conclusion will be to argue that the real villain of the piece might be the Fifth Amendment and the extent of its protection against compelled self-incrimination. Only by understanding the interconnections of these two amendments can one develop cogent views about either.

One of the reasons that we do not protect lovers, best friends, or colleagues from having to give evidence against their associates is that such testimony is often necessary if conviction is to be possible at all. (And, as already noted, the unwillingness of these people to play Judas encourages the use of undercover agents.) The reason for that necessity is relatively simple: we cannot, in the American system of criminal justice, ask a defendant directly to explain the evidence that suggests criminal behavior. Indeed, a juror cannot legally draw any negative inference from the failure of a defendant to testify in his or her own defense.[35]

Society is surely entitled to evidence of criminal behavior directed against it, but the Fifth Amendment prevents direct questioning of the most knowledgeable party about suspected crime, if the person refuses to cooperate. Is there good reason to support this, particularly if the cost includes, as I am suggesting, the seeking of evidence in alternative ways that damage important social values? I think not.

59

The most cogent reasons to support the privilege against self-incrimination have to do with preventing unseemly methods of interrogation, such as physical or psychological brutality; historically, a second reason had to do with the propensity of public officials to ask questions concerning one's views about religious and political doctrines. Both concerns can be adequately handled by means other than a strong privilege against self-incrimination. Under existing positive law, incidentally, the Fifth Amendment cannot be defended as a protector of privacy *per se,* since the state can compel answers to the most painfully incriminating questions so long as it first purchases them by a grant of immunity from criminal prosecution (and thus technically makes the answers "nonincriminating").

One response is that it is an affront to human dignity to force someone to incriminate him- or herself. I do not fully understand this argument, unless it is predicated on an essentially Hobbesian view of society. Indeed, even if we adopt such a stark view, it is unclear why rational social designers of either the Hobbesian or Rawlsian variety would not agree to a general practice of compelled testimony precisely as a means of protecting themselves from their fellows who are presumably motivated by exclusively egoistic considerations.

I agree with Kent Greenawalt's recent argument that, "At least for cases of properly grounded suspicion, the proper basis of a right to silence lies . . . in the notion of compassion. The right should be viewed as a concession to the narrow concerns of most of us, not as an endorsement of that narrowness or a rejection of broader norms of concern and cooperation."[37]

The more important point, however, is that the costs to human dignity of the Fifth Amendment are themselves great. Moreover, the Fifth Amendment was applied to the states only in the 1964 case of *Malloy* v. *Hogan.*[38] It is an irresistible temptation to point out that the so-called "informer trilogy" of 1966 — *Hoffa, Lewis,* and *Osborn* v. *U.S.* — follows almost immediately on the heels of much broader interpretation of the Fifth Amendment by the Supreme Court, the most famous case, of course, being *Miranda* v. *Arizona.*[39] The Court's emphasis on a single uniform standard for both federal and state police under the Fifth Amendment entailed recognition that suppression of undercover activity would be an additional blow to states, which had only recently been brought within the confines of the Amendment at all.

Professor Greenawalt notes the underside of *Miranda*: "Not only are law enforcement officers still able in many cases to take advantage of strong pressures to talk, they may employ strategies, such as the placement of informers . . . that fall well below standards of respect and dignity to which we aspire in most contexts."[40] In response, he calls for the relaxation of constraints currently imposed by the Fifth Amendment, especially the prohibition against taking note of a defendant's pretrial silence. Moreover, he would surround pretrial interrogation with some important safeguards:

> [S]ystematic questioning of a suspect should take place only after probable cause of guilt exists, the point at which arrest is now possible. A neutral official, a magistrate, should determine the presence of probable cause before this more intense questioning occurs. To avoid possible pressure and deceitful manipulation, the questioning should not be done by the police alone, but by a magistrate or in front of him, and the suspect should be afforded counsel. To avoid any subsequent misinterpretation of what took place, a precise record should be kept. At each of these stages, a person would have the privilege of remaining silent . . ., [but] that fact would be introduced as adverse evidence at his trial. If a defendant did not testify at his trial, the jury could be invited by the judge to draw an adverse inference from his silence.[41]

Professor Greenawalt's article can be seen as a consideration of the kinds of tradeoffs that are inevitably part of any criminal justice system that attempts to protect individual dignity and yet solve crimes at the same time. Indeed, one might call for an important "trade"—much more vigorous safeguarding of the interpersonal values currently infringed by the deception inherent in undercover investigations in return for the ability of state and federal police to interrogate directly, under carefully controlled conditions, those they have probable cause to suspect of criminal activity. (Whether or not Greenawalt would endorse such a trade, I certainly do, adding to the agenda the extent of compelled testimony from friends, lovers, and family.)

In the current social mood one may be wary of suggesting such a trade for fear that the diminished Fifth would be eagerly accepted, while nothing would be given in the way of an augmented Fourth. Yet clearly, whatever one's place on the political spectrum, our current regime of public values, including those reflected in law, has scarcely provided adequate solutions to the twin problems of providing society with evidence of wrongs committed against it and protecting our individual privacy and ability to trust one another. Those of us who wish the partisans of unfettered police investigations to re-examine their commitments should be equally willing to place some of our own presuppositions under scrunity.

NOTES

1. Erving Goffman, *Relations in Public* (New York: Basic Books, 1971), pp. 238–333. I am enormously indebted to Goffman's work, as must be anyone who is concerned about the implications of "undercover" work.

2. Stanley Milgram, *Obedience to Authority: An Experimental View* (New York: Harper & Row, 1974) pp. 3–4.

3. Sissela Bok, *Lying* (New York: Pantheon, 1978), p. 18.

4. Anton Chekhov, "The Lady with the Little Dog," quoted in John Bayley, "The Novelist as Pedagogue," *New York Review of Books,* December 3, 1981, p. 19.

5. Charles Fried, *An Anatomy of Values* (Cambridge: Harvard University Press, 1970), p. 142.

6. See Ronald Dworkin, "Liberalism," in Stuart Hampshire, ed., *Public and Private Morality* (Cambridge, England: Cambridge University Press, 1978), pp. 113–143, for a recent influential statement of the thesis that the distinguishing characteristic of liberal political theory is its repudiation of socialization of the citizen into a particular conception of social virtue in favor of an emphasis on individual autonomy.

7. Thomas Hobbes, *Leviathan* (London: Basil Blackwell, 1960), p. 82.

8. Jean Bethke Elshtain, *Public Man, Private Woman: Women in Social and Political Thought* (Princeton: Princeton University Press, 1981), p. 109. Prof. Elshtain's entire book is extremely relevant to the concerns of this essay.

9. This, of course, is one reading of the American Constitution. See, e.g., (James Madison), Federalist No. 51: "If angels were to govern men, neither external nor internal controuls on government would be necessary. In framing a government which is to be administered by men over men, the great difficulty lies in this: You must first enable the government to controul the governed; and the next place, oblige it to controul itself." Jacob Cooke, ed., *The Federalist* (Middletown, Conn.: Wesleyan University Press, 1961), p. 349.

10. See generally Victor Navasky, *Naming Names* (New York: Viking Press, 1980), for a treatment of the role of (and attitudes toward) informers in the 1950s.

11. Michael Walzer, *Obligations* (Cambridge, Mass.: Harvard University Press, 1970), p. 205.

12. Gospel of St. Luke, Chapter 14, Verse 26.
13. See, e.g., the extraordinary book by Robert Daley, *Prince of the City* (Boston: Houghton Mifflin, 1978), detailing the acts (and acting) engaged in by New York detective Robert Leuci. Also worth reading, though without the moral recognition that makes Daley's book exceptional, is Ron Shaffer and Kevin Klose, *Surprise! Surprise! How the Lawmen Conned the Thieves* (New York: Viking Press, 1977), a study of a Washington, D.C., "sting" operation.
14. See Robert Hanley, "Bergen Policy Story: 11 Months as an Underworld Spy," a story which appeared on page one of the New Jersey section of the Sunday *New York Times* sometime, I believe, in the summer of 1976. When I clipped the story, I forgot to include the specific citation, through all quotes came from the Xerox of the original story.
15. One is not sure what "sentimentality" means in this context. The deep and bitter conflict between Irish and British has generated a loathing for those Irish who collaborated with the British. See, for example, the novel by Liam O'Flaherty, *The Informer,* (New York: Alfred A. Knopf, 1925) which was later made into a classic John Ford movie of the same name.
16. Peter Berger, "Now, 'Boat People' from Taiwan?" *New York Times,* February 14, 1978, p. 35.
17. *United States* v. *White,* 401 U.S. 745, 781 (1971) Harlan, J., dissenting).
18. See generally George Dix, "Undercover Investigations and Police Rulemaking," *Texas Law Review 53* (1975), 203–94, for a comprehensive review of the legal literature in regard to control of undercover investigations. See also especially Geoffrey Stone, "The Scope of the Fourth Amendment: Privacy and the Police Use of Spies, Secret Agents, and Informers," *American Bar Foundation Research Journal* (1976), 1193–1271. Three more general studies of the Fourth Amendment are Anthony Amsterdam's magisterial "Perspectives on the Fourth Amendment," *Minnesota Law Review* 58 (1974), 349; Lloyd Weinreb, "The Generalities of the Fourth Amendment," *University of Chicago Law Review* 42 (1974), 47; and James White, "The Fourth Amendment as a Way of Talking About People: A Study of Robinson and Matlock," *1974 Supreme Court Review* (1974), 165.
19. See especially Weinreb. I owe my initial recognition of this point to Prof. Larry Yackle.
20. 373 U.S. 427, 465–466 (1963) (Brennan, J., dissenting).
21. 385 U.S. 293 (1966).
22. *Id.,* at 302.
23. *Id.,* at 302–303.
24. 385 U.S. 206 (1966). Mention should also be made of a third case decided that day, *Osborn* v. *United States,* 385 U.S. 323 (1966), which involved the admissibility of a tape recording of a conversation between an informer and the defendant. What distinguishes *Osborn* from the other two cases is that the taping was authorized by the judges of the local federal district court upon submission of affidavits containing evidence of a specific criminal offense.
25. *Id.,* at 209. Warren quotes the following statement from the Model Penal Code §2.10, comment, p. 16 (Tent. Draft No. 9. 1959): "Particularly, in the enforcement of vice, liquor or narcotics laws, it is all but impossible to obtain evidence for prosecution save by the use of decoys. There are rarely complaining witnesses. The participants in the crime enjoy themselves. Misrepresentation by a police officer or agent concerning the identity of the purchaser of illegal narcotics is a practical necessity . . . Therefore, the law must attempt to distinguish between those deceits and persuasions which are permissable and

those which are not." *Id.,* at 210, ft. 6.

26. *Id.,* at 210.
27. White, *supra* note 18, at 230.
28. See particularly *U.S.* v. *White,* 401 U.S. 745 (1971).
29. As George Dix points out, "If the requirement of probable cause were applied accurately, law enforcement agencies would need grounds to arrest the subject for past offenses before they could begin the undercover investigation. This unrealistic position is inconsistent with the attractive notion that evidentiary standards required of police should increase as the investigation proceeds. Grounds for arrest should not be required for an investigation that is clearly intended to precede arrest." "Undercover Investigations," *Texas Law Review,* p. 223, footnote 34.
30. 100 S. Ct. 906 (1980).
31. See Wayne King, "Girl Refuses to Testify Against Mother Before a Grand Jury in Las Vegas," *New York Times,* March 12, 1981, p. 10.
32. Dix, "Undercover Investigations," p. 211.
33. See Deirdre Carmody, "Exposure of Corruption Raises Questions About Reporters' Masquerading," *New York Times,* February 23, 1978, p. A16.
34. Quoted in Dix, "Undercover Investigations," pp. 211–12, footnote 9.
35. See *Griffin* v. *California,* 380 U.S. 609 (1965).
36. See *Ullmann* v. *United States.* 350 U.S. 422 (1956); *Kastigar* v. *United States,* 406, U.S. 441 (1972).
37. Kent Greenawalt, "The Right to Silence," *William and Mary Law Review* 15 (1981), 50.
38. 373 U.S. 1 (1964).
39. 384 U.S. 436 (1966).
40. Greenawalt, "The Right to Silence," p. 68.
41. *Ibid.,* p. 51.

4

Who Really Gets Stung?
Some Issues Raised by
the New Police Undercover Work

Gary T. Marx*

RECENT FEDERAL INVESTIGATIONS, SUCH AS ABSCAM, MILAB, and BRILAB, and the many local variations, such as police-run fencing fronts and anticrime decoy squads, call attention to changes in an old police tactic: undercover work. In the last decade, covert law enforcement activity has expanded in scale and changed in form. At the local

* Reprinted with permission from *Crime & Delinquency,* April 1982, pp. 165–193.

level, for example, the proportion of all police arrests involving under-cover work has roughly doubled in the last 15 years. This represents in part an increase in work countering drug offenses. But new federal aid for strike forces, the Witness Protection Program, fencing stings, and anticrime decoys has been a major stimulus. With increased attention given to organized and white collar crime, the Federal Bureau of Investigation has dropped J. Edgar Hoover's policy of prohibiting sworn agents from playing undercover roles. Funding for FBI undercover operations increased from $1 million to $4.8 million from 1978 to 1981. Recent FBI investigations into political corruption, insurance fraud, and labor racke-teering have received extensive media attention. Moreover, other govern-ment agencies in addition to law enforcement appear to be making increased use of undercover tactics as part of their audit and general inspection procedures.

Undercover tactics have, of course, been used for vice and political crimes since the turn of the century; yet, within professional police cir-cles, these tended to be seen as insignificant and marginal activities. These traditional undercover practices have been supplemented by new and more complex forms and changing emphasis and attitudes.

Undercover work is increasingly viewed as an important and inno-vative police tactic carried out by carefully chosen, elite units. In many big-city police departments, competition for assignment to such units, such as anticrime decoy squads, is intense: Assignment to tactical or special squads which use undercover tactics in new ways brings increased prestige and professional recognition. Their use has been extended to white collar corruption and street offenses, and to consumers of activities constituting vice crimes (reaching beyond the customary targets, the providers of those activities). Examples of the latter can be seen in decoy police women posing as prostitutes and arresting men who proposition them, and undercover officers offering to sell (rather than buy) drugs. The lone undercover worker making isolated arrests has been supple-mented or replaced by highly coordinated and staged team activities, involving technological aids and many agents and arrests. Informers have always been central to undercover work for information, introduc-tion, and often participation. Recent complex undercover operations have relied heavily upon unwitting informers, persons unaware that they

66

were part of a police operation, and who therefore were not bound by the legal and administrative restrictions under which police operate.

With such consensual crimes as prostitution or gambling, the undercover transaction has been restricted to the consenting adults involved. But recent undercover work in other types of consensual crimes (such as the buying and selling of stolen property, with police posing as fences) may entail victimization of third parties. Goals and targeting have also changed. Traditionally, undercover work has been used in a targeted fashion as part of a criminal investigation after a crime has occurred, where there is a suspect and his apprehension is the goal. Today, its range is broader, as undercover work has become part of efforts to anticipate crimes not yet committed, where there is as yet no suspect, and where deterrence is an important goal.

There is neither a single nor a simple reason for changes in the nature and scale of undercover work. Multiple factors are involved, and they interact in complex ways. At a very general level, there appears to be a decline in the acceptance of coercive means to control people, with a concomitant rise in deceptive means. Values of rational organization, planning, and prevention are increasingly important in varied institutions, whether medical, educational, or criminal justice.

For those concerned with criminal justice reform, one of the most interesting issues involves the possible link between the success of demands to change police priorities and limit past abuses by police and increases in undercover work. In the case of the former, the FBI's new white collar and organized crime priorities led easily to increased undercover work as an effective tactic for dealing with consensual or skilled offenders.

While rightfully focusing on continuing abuses and some retreat from earlier gains, civil libertarians can note considerable progress with respect to some aspects of police reform. The legal environment in which police work has changed markedly in recent decades. While the new limitations they face can easily be exaggerated, it is clear that the conditions of police work have altered. The rights guaranteed citizens under the Constitution are better honored than in the past. Supreme Court decisions, legislation, and departmental policies have restricted the conditions under which police can gather information, whether through search and seizure, electronic surveillance, or stressful and coercive interrogation after arrest. Police must build stronger cases in order to arrest and convict, and there is less tolerance in the courts of extralegal techniques for effecting an apprehension.

One response to the exclusionary rule, *Miranda, Escobido,* and the like, is for police simply to do less for fear of running afoul of departmental and court rulings. But another is to seek imaginative ways around the rulings, as in the increased use of informants and undercover work involving anticrime decoys, false fencing fronts, and infiltration. There need be little problem with rules of evidence, interrogations, the search for a suspect, testimony, and guilt if the undercover officer is a direct party to the offense, and the crime has even been videotaped in living color. Better still if (as was the case with ABSCAM) an assistant attorney general or prosecutor can monitor the videotape as the action unfolds and even place a call to undercover agents warning them if their behavior verges on entrapment.

As the police use of coercion has been restricted, their use of deception has increased. Restricting police investigation after a crime occurs has increased the attention paid to anticipating crimes. Restricting the conditions under which the police can carry out searches and seizures, participate in violence or felonies, or engage in coercive persuasion as part of undercover investigations has meant increased use of civilians (knowing and unwitting informants, private detectives), who are less accountable than the police. Thus, increased police respect for individual liberties and rights may come partly at a cost of widening manipulation of citizens by informants and other civilians used by law enforcement. What police want to have done but cannot themselves do legally may be delegated to others.

This ironic link between reform and the spread of undercover practices is an intriguing example of the unintended consequences of reform, a topic that is finally beginning to receive the serious academic attention it deserves.[1]

As police departments have become more bureaucratic, modern management techniques have been adopted. For example, one can see a greater emphasis on measuring output as a means of accountability and an attempt to anticipate and sometimes even create demand. Increased conflict with minorities and the politically and culturally disenchanted may also have made it more difficult for the police to gain crime information or to obtain complaints or testimony from alienated or intimidated citizens. This also means greater reliance on informers and undercover work to gain information and witnesses.

New crime problems are also important. The increase in street crime over the last decade has led to the search for better methods of crime control. The spread of organized crime's activities has stimulated expanded and more sophisticated undercover work, as have the proliferation of heroin and other serious drugs and establishment of sophisticated international distribution networks.

Beyond the provision of new federal financial resources and guidance for undercover work, technical innovations appear to be relevant. The development of highly intrusive and easily hidden surveillance technology has encouraged undercover work. But whatever is responsible for the changes in undercover investigation, it is clear that important policy questions are at stake. Executive and legislative bodies responsible for general police policy and accountability, courts, police managers, and policy analysts have not adequately confronted these questions.

The advantages and successes of recent undercover work have been well publicized. For example, for certain offenses, such as bribery and drug sales, the tactic can permit arrests rarely possible using overt methods. This is also the case for crimes in which a well-organized, skilled, or particularly intimidating group is involved. Knowledge that anyone on the street could be a police officer may deter some offenders and increase feelings of safety among citizens. Conviction rates are high when an undercover officer has been party to a crime, and even higher when videotaped evidence is presented. And the courts' willingness to accept complex undercover activities such as ABSCAM as legal has diverted attention from problematic questions.

Given the favorable press that recent undercover work has generally received and the secrecy that surrounds such operations (the relative ease with which agents may overlook or disguise mistakes, abuses, and costs), the public perceptions probably reflect an overestimation of the advantages and underestimation of the disadvantages of the tactic. The mere fact that a practice is legal should not be sufficient grounds for its use. Its ethical, practical, economic, and social implications must also be considered. Without denying the positive aspects of undercover work or arguing that it should be categorically prohibited, I will discuss some disadvantages, costs, and risks which have received inadequate public attention. I also wish to offer reasons why undercover tactics can be more troubling than overt police methods, and, as a result, require greater restrictions and closer supervision. Determining the frequency of unintended consequences of undercover work and weighing the competing values and trade-offs are important tasks for research and policy analysis, and much work remains to be done. Identifying the issues at stake is a crucial first step. I will consider these as they bear upon targets of the investigation, informers, police, third parties, and society in general.[2]

Targets: Trickery, Coercion, Temptation

In considering the targets of undercover investigations, European observers are often surprised at how far American police are permitted to go in generating conditions for crime. The law and courts are very tolerant here. Recent decisions, such as those in the Hoffa, Lewis, Osborne, Russell, Hampton and Twigg cases,[3] continue this support. The predisposition of the offender, rather than the objective methods of police, tends to be seen as the key factor in determining entrapment at the federal level. The fact that the crime could not or would not have occurred had the government not been involved is usually not considered legally relevant if the person is thought to have been predisposed to engage in the prohibited activity. Yet, for understanding causes of behavior, and developing guidelines for the use of scarce law enforcement resources, issues related to the behavior of government agents is crucial. The fact that a tactic is legal does not necessarily imply that its use is ethical. In addition, because of the secrecy surrounding undercover work, it can easily be used in ways that are illegal. This section considers issues bearing on the targets of undercover operations.

Three types of agent behavior are of particular interest: the use of excessive trickery, the use of coercion, and the offer of extraordinarily seductive temptations. Where the behavior of the undercover agent exhibits any of these characteristics, it may be questionable whether the suspect acted with autonomy and full knowledge of the illegal nature of his behavior. Let us consider each of the above.

Trickery

Three common forms of trickery are (1) offering the illegal action as a minor part of a very attractive socially legitimate goal, (2) hiding or disguising the illegal nature of the action, and (3) weakening the capacity of the target to distinguish right and wrong (or choosing a suspect who is already so weakened). In the first case, targets are lured into the activity on a pretext. The goal put forth is legal and desirable, and the illegality is secondary. Thus, in the most questionable ABSCAM case, that in Philadelphia, the defendants were told that their involvement could bring a convention center and possibly other means of financial gain to the city. They were led to believe that the project would not come to Philadelphia if they did not accept the money. Judge Fullam, in his ruling on the Philadelphia case of Schwartz and Jannotte, indicates that neither of the defendants asked for money and both indicated that no payment was necessary.[4]

In another example, Rommie Loudd, the first black executive with a professional sports team, organized the Orlando, Florida, franchise in the World Football League. With the failure of the league, Loudd went broke. A man whom he did not know called and offered him $1 million to reorganize his team. The caller promised to bring wealthy colleagues into the deal, but Loudd was told he first had to loosen up the financiers with cocaine. He resisted the offer, but eventually introduced the caller (an undercover agent) to two people who sold him cocaine. Loudd, with no previous criminal record, was sentenced to a long prison term. On tape, the agent involved said to his partner, "I've tricked him worse than I've tricked anybody ever."[5]

Ignorance of the law is, of course, not an excuse for its violation. However, the situation seems different (at least, ethically) when one is led into illegal activities by a government agent who claims that no wrongdoing is occurring. Here the agent creates a subterfuge in order to make it appear to the suspect that nothing illegal is happening.

In several ABSCAM cases, defendants were led to believe that they could make money without having to deliver any promises. The videotape from the case of New Jersey Senator Harrison Williams reveals the main informant coaching the senator in what to say, almost putting words in his mouth: "You gotta tell him how important you are, and you gotta tell him in no uncertain terms— 'without me, there is no deal. I'm the man who's gonna open the doors. I'm the man who's gonna do this and use my influence and I guarantee this.'" The senator is then assured that nothing wrong is happening: "It goes no further. It's all talk, all bullshit. It's a walk-through. You gotta just play and blow your horn."[6]

Some ABSCAM defendants were told that, in accordance with the "Arab mind" and "Arab way of doing business," they must convince the investors that they had friends in high places. In order to do this, money had to be accepted from the apparent investors, although the defendants were not required by the undercover agents to offer any commitments contingent on accepting the payment. The key element was appearances. In Philadelphia, the situation was structured so that the acceptance of money would be seen as payment for private consulting services and not as the acceptance of a bribe.[7] The defendants were not asked to behave improperly.

Another problematic situation involves the use of trickery against people with diminished capacity, such as the mentally limited or ill, juveniles, and persons under extreme pressure or in a needy or weakened state (e.g., addicts in withdrawal). Such persons may be more susceptible to persuasion and less able than most citizens to distinguish right from wrong. As part of the investigation, the undercover agent may attempt to create or may aggravate such conditions in the target. Rep. Thompson refused the first offer of cash. However, he eventually took money after resourceful government agents (who had concluded that he was an alcoholic) gave him liquor.

Coercion

Participation may stem from a fear of the failure to cooperate rather than from free choice. An element of this seems inherent in certain sham criminal situations, or in employing as informants those accustomed to using threats of violence to get their way.

For example, two federal agents and a convicted armed robber became involved in a gambling and prostitution front in Alaska. This was part of an anticipatory plan to deal with organized crime, believed to

72

be coming into the area because of opportunities offered by the pipeline project. The agents helped finance a bar which was to be the center of the operation and actively sought participants for the scheme. One of the agents posed as the organization's "heavy muscle"—and appears to have played a heavy-handed role in intimidating and prodding some participants.[8]

In a case growing out of a Washington, D.C., fencing sting, former assistant United States attorney Donald Robinson was accused of taking money for information from persons he thought were organized crime figures, but who were actually police. He eventually won his case on the grounds of entrapment. Robinson had at first ignored their approaches, but became involved after persistent telephone calls, a threatening call to his wife, and a warning that he might end up missing.[9] When coercion is mixed with temptation, the incentive to participate can be very strong.

Temptation

Recent undercover actions have transformed the Biblical injunction to something like, "lead us into temptation and deliver us from evil." Temptation raises different issues than coercion or trickery. An act is no less criminal because it is engaged in as a response to a very attractive temptation than if it is committed without the presentation of temptation. The concerns raised are instead the assumptions on which the tactic is based, the questionable fairness of such a technique, and whether scarce resources ought to be used to pose temptation.

Defenders of these tactics usually make the assumption that the world is divided clearly between criminal and noncriminal citizens. It is assumed that presenting a temptation will not endanger the uprightness of the latter, while the former will commit the offense if given any opportunity to do so. Numerous critics have questioned this, noting the importance in criminality of situational factors. A well-known story captures something of this disagreement regarding the nature of motivation to engage in deviant behavior. A man encounters a woman in a fancy bar and asks her, "Would you accompany me to my hotel room for $10,000?" She says yes. Whereupon he asks her whether she would come to his room for $10. She indignantly says, "No, what kind of a girl do you think I am?" He responds, "Madam, we have already established that, what we are haggling about is the price." Depending on the side taken in this story, deviance is seen as either an inherent or a conditional attribute.

Of course, much depends on the type of offense. For some, the line between the criminal and noncriminal can be easily blurred through the offer of secret temptations. Al Capone captured this insight (if going too far) when, in response to a reporter's question, he said something like, "Lady, when you get down to cases, nobody's on the legit." Or, put differently in the immortal words of Mel Weinberg, the key figure in the ABSCAM case, "You put the big honeypot out there, all the flies come to it."

It is certainly not true that everyone has his price or can be tempted. The imagery of turning on a faucet or providing sticky flypaper is overdrawn. However, there are certain types of behavior in which undercover tactics can turn up offenses a goodly proportion of the time among persons not thought of as criminals. This is the case for sexual encounters, underage drinking, marijuana use, minor traffic violations, and certain forms of illegality related to routine job performance. For example, a building inspector or purchasing agent may take a bribe or accept a gift for issuing a permit or purchasing goods that would have been issued or bought anyway; merchants and manufacturers will buy needed goods very cheaply without asking questions; and it is usually little problem to sell consumers goods such as televisions and stereos when offered at big discounts. The number of arrests possible from certain undercover actions is astounding. In situations were illegality is so easy to generate, the secret provision of state opportunities should be handled in accordance with a clear set of priorities with respect to both types of offense and offender. The necessity to make the best use of scarce resources, as well as fairness, requires that seriousness rather than the technical ease of making a case be a major criterion governing law enforcement's uses of culpability.

When there is a well-documented pattern of prior serious infractions or reasons for suspicion, secret testing may be appropriate. It may also be appropriate for persons in positions of special trust or temptation, if they are warned beforehand that the tactic may be used. But there is a danger that, once resources are provided and skills developed, the tactic

74

will be abused. It may have been appropriate for God to test Job. The conditions under which it is appropriate for humans to test one another need careful specification. Some of the new police undercover work has lost sight of the profound difference between carrying out an investigation to determine whether a suspect is, in fact, breaking the law, and carrying it out to determine whether an individual *can be induced* to break the law. As with God's testing of Job, the question "Is he corrupt?" may be replaced with the question "Is he corruptible?" Questions of police discretion are involved here. With limited resources, how much attention should authorities devote to crimes that appear in response to the opportunity they themselves generate or that can be subtly ferreted out through secret tactics, rather than focusing on offenses that appear without their inducement? As Justice Frankfurter wrote in *Sherman* v. *U.S.*, "Human nature is weak enough and sufficiently beset by temptations without the government adding to them and generating crime."[10]

Even if temptations are not offered, most complex activities, whether of businessmen, legislators, or academics, have legally gray areas wherein secret investigations could turn up violations. In many bureaucratic settings, "creative bookkeeping" may be illegal or at least violate internal policy, but organizational functioning would be much inhibited without it. Those who get ahead in organizations are often the persons who make things happen by breaking, bending, and twisting rules and by cutting through red tape. Rules are often general, contradictory, and open to varied interpretations. As those in law enforcement bureaucracies know too well, organizations have a vast number of rules that are overlooked until a supervisor wants to find fault with someone. In such cases, morality and conformity are often not the simple phenomena that the record of rule violation may make them out to be. The use of secret forms of information gathering, without there even being temptations, can thus be problematic.

Political Targeting and Misuse of Results

The vagaries and complexities of motivation aside, questions can also be raised about how targets are chosen and how the results of an investigation are used. Undercover operations can be contrasted with conventional investigations which appear in response to the complaint of a victim. The latter offer some controls not present in secret investigations undertaken at police initiative. Openness in an investigation (with respect to the fact that it is being carried out and the means used to do so) and the presence of a complainant as a concerned outside party reduce discretionary power. Secret investigations carried out at police initiative that involve testing of integrity are a powerful means for the discovery or creation of discrediting information. They can offer a powerful way to control a person through arrest, the threat of exposure, or damage to a reputation through leaks of information. The potential for political and personal misuse of undercover work appears to be greater than that with overt police methods.

The last decade offers many examples of undercover targeting of radical activists, who could not be arrested for their political beliefs, for drug and other arrests. In Los Angeles, a top mayoral aid, unpopular with police because of his role in police department changes, was arrested on a morals charge under questionable circumstances. He lost his job.

Even persons who reject an undercover temptation may still be harmed. Involvement as a suspect in the apparatus of a covert government investigation cannot help but cast a shadow on a person's reputation. To be secretly videotaped or tape recorded and then to have this made public will convey a presumption of guilt to the uncritical. For the unprincipled, undercover tactics may offer a tool for character assassination.

Investigations may be carried out with no intention of formal prosecution. In cases where there is no prosecution because of insufficient evidence, rejection of the offer, or improper official behavior, the subject may still be damaged through leaks to the media. The government's unregulated power to carry out integrity tests at will offers a means of slander, regardless of the outcome of the test. In the case of politicians, for whom matters of public reputation are central, the issue is particularly salient. The breadth of some criminal laws (e.g., conspiracy) in the absence of internal guidelines gives police wide discretion in deciding whom to investigate. This routine discretion can mask the political motivation that may be behind an investigation.

As with other privacy-invading tactics, such as electronic surveillance or access to confidential records, there is the potential in undercover work for blackmail and coercion. Information gained may never be used in court, but may be filed away as long as those implicated continue to cooperate with the controlling agent—in legal ways, such as by offering information or setting up others, or in illegal ways, such as through pay-offs.[11] Getting information on the extent of this type of coercion is very difficult, since undercover police and those blackmailed have a shared conspirational interest in keeping silent.

In some jurisdictions where employees are required to report illegal activities, they may face double testing. Thus, an employee of New York City's Buildings Department was approached by an undercover investigator who offered him a bribe if he would submit falsified architectural plans. The bribe was rejected. However, the inspector was suspended from his job for failing to report the bribe attempt.[12] Although legal, this action takes the traditional integrity test to a new extreme. A person may become the target of an undercover opportunity scheme, not because of suspected corruption, but merely to see whether requirements that bribes be reported are followed. The potential for misuse is clear. This technique can be a tool for getting rid of employees seen as troublesome for other reasons.

Effects on Police

Undercover work offers great risks and temptations to the police involved. As is the case with informants, the secrecy of the situation, the protected access to illegality, and the usual absence of a complainant can be conducive to corruption and abuse. As noted, undercover operations can offer a way for agents to make easy cases or to retaliate, damage, or gain leverage against suspects not otherwise liable to prosecution. Issues of entrapment, blackmail, and leaks were considered in the section on targets. Here the focus is on direct implications for police.

The character of police work, with its isolation, secrecy, discretion, uncertainty, temptations, and need for suspicion, is frequently drawn upon to explain (1) poor relations between police and the community, (2) the presence of a police subculture in conflict with formal departmental policy, and (3) police stress symptoms. These characteristics are even more pronounced in the case of undercover work, which also involves other factors that may be conducive to a variety of problems. Beyond the threat of physical danger from discovery, there may be severe social and psychological consequences for police who play undercover roles for an extended period of time.

Undercover situations tend to be more fluid and unpredictable than is the case with routine patrol or investigative work. There is greater autonomy for agents, and rules and procedures are less clear. The expenses in setting up an undercover operation are often significant; thus, the financial costs of mistakes or failure are much higher than in conventional investigations. The need for secrecy accentuates problems of coordination and concern over the great potential for error. Undercover police may unknowingly enforce the law against one another or have it enforced against themselves, sometimes with tragic consequences.

Undercover agents are removed from the usual controls of a uniform, a badge, a visible supervisor, a fixed place of work, radio or beeper calls, and a delineated assignment. These have both a literal and a symbolic significance in reminding the officer who he or she is.

Unlike conventional police work, activities by the undercover agent tend to involve only criminals, and the agent is always carrying out deception; thus, a criminal environment and role models assume predominance in the officer's working life. The agent is encouraged to pose as a criminal. His ability to blend in, to resemble criminals, and to be accepted is central to effectiveness. It also serves as an indication to the agent that he or she is doing a good job. As positive personal relationships develop, the agent may experience guilt, and ambivalence may develop over the betrayal inherent in the deceptive role being played. The work is very intense; the agent is always "on." For some agents, the work becomes almost addicting, as they come to enjoy the sense of power the role offers and its protected contact with illegal activity.

Isolation from other contacts and the need to be liked and accepted by members of a criminal subculture can have unintended consequences. "Playing the crook" may increase cynicism and ambivalence about the police role and make it easier to rationalize the use of illegal and immoral means, whether for agency or for corrupt goals. In his novel *Mother-Night*, Vonnegut tells us that "we are what we pretend to be, so we must be careful about what we pretend to be."[13] Police may become consumers or purveyors of the very vice they set out to control.

A good example of this can be seen in the case of a northern California police officer who participated in a "deep cover" operation for a year and a half, riding with the Hell's Angels. He was responsible for a very large number of arrests, including heretofore almost untouchable high-level drug dealers, and was praised for doing a "magnificent job." But this came at a cost of heavy drug use, alcoholism, brawling, the break-up of his family, an inability to fit back into routine police work after the investigation was over, resignation from the force, several bank robberies, and a prison term.[14]

Other examples include a Chicago police officer whose undercover work involved posing as a pimp and infiltrating a prostitution ring. He continued in the pimp role after the investigation ended and was suspended.[15] A member of an elite drug enforcement unit in the Boston area became an addict and retired on a disability pension.[16]

The financial rewards from police corruption, particularly in gambling and narcotics, can be great and the chances of avoiding detection rather good. Ironically, effectiveness and opportunities for corruption may often go hand in hand.[17] Police supervisors and lawbreakers may face equal difficulties in knowing what undercover police officers are really up to. Awareness of the problematic aspects of undercover activity helps explain J. Edgar Hoover's opposition to having sworn agents in such roles. The stellar reputation of the FBI for integrity is attributable, in part, to Hoover's refusal to allow the agents to face the temptations confronting police in agencies routinely involved in undercover activities.

Other costs to police, while not raising ethical or legal issues, can be wasted resources and even tragic consequences. The secrecy, presence of multiple enforcement agencies, and nature of many undercover activities can mean that police end up enforcing the law against one another. Sometimes the instances are merely comical, as in the case described by Whited.[18] Here, an effeminate man wearing mascara went for a walk with another man he met at a gay bar. After a series of suggestive comments, the former, an undercover officer, sought to arrest his companion. He discovered that the companion, also an undercover officer, was hoping to arrest him. Other times, however, the results are far more serious, as undercover police are shot or killed by other police. In recent years in the New York area alone, eight black police officers in undercover roles or working as plainclothes officers have been shot (five fatally) by other police officers who mistook them for lawbreakers.[19]

Informers

Exploitation of the system by informers can be a major problem. The frequency and seriousness of the problems informers can cause make them the weakest link in undercover systems. But most undercover operations must rely to some degree on such persons in the criminal milieu for information, technical advice, "clients," contacts, and introductions involving legitimation of the agents' own disreputability. A heavy price may be paid for this. Although informers face exceptional risks, they also face exceptional opportunities.

Some recent cases appear to represent a significant delegation of law enforcement investigative authority. Informers can be offered a license to pursue whatever target they choose, as long as they assert that the person selected is predisposed to commit illegal actions. Verification of such assertions is often difficult. Control agents are dependent on persons whose professional lives routinely involve deceit and concealment. When the informer has a motive to lie, as is often the case, matters are even worse. Because of charges they are seeking to avoid, the promise of drugs or money, or a desire to punish competitors or enemies, informers may have strong incentives to see that others break the law. This can mean false claims about past misbehavior of targets and ignoring legal and departmental restrictions. Whether out of self-interest or deeper psychological motives, some informers undergo a transformation and become zealous super-cops, creating criminals or sniffing them out using prohibited methods.

The convicted swindler in ABSCAM (described by Judge Fullam as an "archetypical, amoral, fast-buck artist") had a three-year prison sentence waived and received $133,150 for his cooperation in the two-year investigation. Accounts in an internal Justice Department memorandum indicate that he "would be paid a lump sum at the end of ABSCAM, contingent upon the success of the prosecution." In testimony at Representative John Jenrette's trial, the informer acknowledged that he expects to make more than $200,000 from his undercover activities. He also received a $15,000 advance for a book on his exploits.[20] In an age where

80

"books by crooks" (not to mention movies and the lecture circuit) can mean big money, informers have a further incentive for dramatic discoveries.

The bridge to the truth and respect for law may be further weakened when brokers or middlemen are drawn into the operation. The latter do not even know they are part of a police operation. For example, a device used by some fencing stings is to employ street persons to spread the word that a new fence is paying good prices. A commission is paid the unwitting informer for each transaction he is responsible for. The informer may also collect a fee from the person selling the property. One of the most troubling aspects of many of the ABSCAM cases is the role played by middlemen. For example, Joseph Silvestri, one such middleman, was apparently led to believe that he could earn a $6 million broker's fee for helping an Arab sheik invest $60 million in real estate. A condition for his earning the fee was gaining the cooperation of political figures, to be sure that all would work smoothly. It is not surprising that he apparently cast a wide net in seeking to gain "cooperation" from public officials.[21] Claims about past misbehavior or the predisposition of potential targets become even more suspect when this circuitous path is followed. This may help account for why, under the very tempting conditions of ABSCAM, it appears that only half of those approached took the bait.

Informers and, to an even greater extent, middlemen are formally much less accountable than are sworn law officers and are not as constrained by legal or departmental restrictions. As an experienced undercover agent candidly put it, "Unwitting informers are desirable precisely because they can do what we can't—legally entrap." This need not involve police telling informers to act illegally. But the structure of the situation, with its insulation from observability, skills at deception, and strong incentives on the part of the informer, makes supervision very difficult. Videotapes and recordings are a means of monitoring informer behavior. But the crucial and generally unknowable issue is what takes place off the tape recording. To what extent are events on the tape contrived? Informers and middlemen are well situated to engage in entrapment and the fabrication of evidence. Furthermore, the structure of the situation may enable informers to commit crimes of their own, apart from their role as law enforcement agents.

The informer-controller relationship is usually seen to involve the latter exercising coercion over the former. Through a kind of institutionalized blackmail—the threat of jail or public denouncement as an informer—prosecution is held in abeyance as long as cooperation is forthcoming. What is less frequently realized is that the situation can be reversed. When not able to hide criminal behavior, the skilled or fortunately situated informer may be able to manipulate or coerce the controller as well, with neither able to react.

The relationship can be exploited in other ways. Informers may secretly and selectively "give up" sworn undercover agents. The informer's knowledge of police can be a resource traded within criminal milieus. Or informers may sell the same information to several law enforcement agencies, in each case concealing the similar transactions with the other agencies. This leads to the possibility of confrontations between the undercover agents from different agencies who are unaware of each other's identity.

The price of gaining the cooperation of informers may be the necessity to ignore their rule breaking. But beyond this "principled nonenforcement," these situations lend themselves well to exploitation by informers for their own criminal ends. Major cases may require the government to deal with master con artists operating in their natural habitat. They are likely to have a competitive edge over police.

An insurance expert playing an undercover role in "operation frontload," investigating organized crime in the construction industry, was apparently able to obtain $300,000 in fees and issued worthless insurance "performance bonds." As part of his cover, he was certified as an agent of the New Hampshire Insurance Group with the power to issue bonds. The problems in this expensive case, which resulted in no indictments, became known through a suit against the government.[22] How many other such cases are there that we do not hear about because no one brings suit?

An informer in the ABSCAM case was apparently able to exploit his role and the false front that had been set up (Abdul Enterprises, Ltd.) to swindle West Coast businessmen. Realizing they had been taken, the businessmen complained to the FBI. However, the informer was able to

82

carry on for a year and a half. The FBI took no action, essentially covering up his crime until after ABSCAM became public.[23]

Here we see a type of immunity that undercover work may offer. In this case, it was only temporary, serving to protect the secrecy of an ongoing investigation. Once the investigation was over, the informer was indicted, although one can speculate on the harm done (and lack of compensation) to the victims. Their victimization was indirectly aided by the government, first through its helping to provide the opportunity and then in its failing to intervene to warn others. Even more troubling are cases in which informers can essentially blackmail police into granting them permanent immunity. This happens when a trial and related publicity would reveal dirty tricks and illegality on the part of government agents, secret sources, techniques of operation, projects, or classified information

A related phenomenon is crimes committed by persons who have been given new identities and relocated as a result of the federal Witness Protection Program. The fact that such persons may eventually be prosecuted does not detract from the damage caused to third parties through the government's indirect complicity. Furthermore, prosecution for later crimes is not assured, either because of the witnesses' continuing usefulness, because of what they know, or because of the nature of the offense. For example, no matter what kind of bad debts (including unpaid child support) protected witnesses incur using their phony credentials, the Justice Department apparently will not reveal their identity. A relocated witness may even be moved again and again. Graham cites the example of a witness provided with a new identity who was relocated from Oklahoma to Minnesota to North Carolina, to protect him from the bad debts he continually ran up.[24] The ethical and practical consequences of helping career criminals relocate with a false identity in the midst of an unsuspecting community have received little attention.

Third Parties

The possible damage to third parties is one of the least explored aspects of undercover work. Because of the secrecy and second-order ripple effects, much of the damage never comes to public attention. Those who are hurt may not even be aware of it to complain or seek damages. Its invisibility makes the harm even more problematic.

One type of damage to third parties has already been considered, crimes committed by informers under the protection of their role, but unrelated to an investigation. A second type more directly involves the intended law enforcement role. The most obvious cases involve the victims of government-inspired or facilitated crimes. These may be of a collateral nature, as in a Lakewood, Colorado, case, where two young men learned that a local "fence"—in reality a police sting—was buying stolen cars. They stole several cars and sold them to the sting. They showed the undercover officers a .45 caliber automatic taken in a burglary, stole another car, killed its owner in the process with this gun, and then sold the car to the "fence." They repeated this again and were then arrested.[25]

According to one estimate, only about half the property stolen for the purpose of sale to a police-run fencing operation is actually returned to its owners.[26] People may not report their loss, or the property may lack distinctive identification. Even when people do get their property back, it can be argued that the trauma of their victimization should entitle them to some special compensation because of the government's role.

For security reasons or to gain compliance, citizens or businesses approached about cooperating with an undercover operation may not be given the full and candid account necessary for truly informed consent. Such was apparently the case with the informer in "operation frontload." In seeking his certification as an insurance agent with the power to issue bonds, FBI agents described him to the insurance company in question as a former police officer and "a straight arrow," and used a false name. The insurance company was not told of his criminal record, nor of the fact that he had agreed to be an informer to avoid a nine-year prison sentence and a fine. Because of the misbehavior of this informer, as of May 1979 damage suits had been filed in five states against the New Hampshire Insurance Group, the certifying insurance company. Company officials claim that his actions in issuing fake performance bonds to construction companies cost them and insurance brokers more than $60 million in business losses. The head of a Chicago insurance firm states, "What the FBI did was a disgrace . . . They've ruined us." He is suing for $40 million.[27]

84

The web of human interdependence is dense, and by trifling with one part of it for deceptive purposes one may send out reverberations that are no less damaging for being unseen. Have any small businesses been hurt by the competition from proprietary fronts run by police? To appear legitimate, such fronts may actually become competitors during the investigation. Government agents with their skills and no need to make a profit would seem to have an obvious competitive edge over many small businessmen.

The damage to third parties need not be only economic. The most private and delicate of human emotions and relationships may be violated under the mantle of government deceit. As part of an attempt to infiltrate the Weather Underground, a federal agent developed a relationship with a woman. She became pregnant. After considerable indecision and at the urging of the agent, she decided to have an abortion. The agent's work then took him elsewhere and he ended the relationship, with the woman apparently never knowing his secret identity and true motives.[28] One can imagine the publicity and law suits if she had kept the child and the circumstances of the paternity had become known, or if she had died in childbirth, or become mentally unstable.

Another form of damage to innocent third parties may lie in the harmful publicity resulting from having their names mentioned on tapes which become public. This was the case for at least three senators mentioned as possible targets for ABSCAM. The frequent reliance of such investigations on con artists with a proclivity to lie, boast, and exaggerate is conducive to colorful and damaging exchanges or mistaken investigation. The fact that a person wrongly named by an informer may later receive a letter from the Justice Department indicating that an intensive investigation "disclosed no evidence of illegality that warranted our further investigation" seems small compensation once he has been implicitly tried by the newspapers.

While likely infrequent, another problem involves "good samaritans" who happen upon undercover operations and take action through benign motives which police may misinterpret. In a Boston case, for example, two college students heard a woman scream and intervened in what they thought was a crime in progress. They were then arrested and charged with assault and battery and helping a prisoner escape. The "crime" involved a decoy squad trying to arrest the woman's male companion.[29] In New York, a minister and a former medical student were arrested as a result of what they claimed was an effort to help a "drunk" decoy with an exposed wallet. Charges were dropped. The minister reported feeling shaken and humiliated. He spent 13 hours in custody after trying to aid the apparently unconscious decoy.[30]

Such occurrences are probably rare, but given the lack of systematic research, one cannot maintain this with certainty. The need to meet arrest quotas and desire to protect the decoy from assault may mean immediate police action once a person bends over or touches a sprawled decoy. This means that arrest of persons without criminal intent will occur.

Indirect damage to third parties may be seen in a possible increase in police impersonators as undercover work becomes more prevalent. Impersonators are offered role models and their initial tales made more credible by the public's knowledge that undercover work is common. Classic con games, such as the game in which the "mark" is persuaded to draw money from his bank in order to test secretly the honesty of bank employees, may be made more believable by public knowledge that various kinds of secret government integrity tests are carried out. Official statistics probably greatly underestimate the extent of police imperson-ation, since the persons preyed upon are often prostitutes, homosexuals, and persons seeking to buy or sell narcotics, who are relatively unlikely to report their victimization.

Conventional Measures of Effectiveness

In assessing the consequences of undercover work with respect to crime, a distinction should be made between operations directed against subjects whose identity is known in advance, as with the infiltration of particular organizations, the disguise of police as hit men, or the offer of an opportunity for corruption to a person under suspicion, and opera-tions directed against a more general "market" of suspects, as with decoys and fencing stings. The former type of undercover work is judged by its success in the case in question. Was a serious crime prevented? Were convictions obtained that would not have been possible with con-ventional methods? The goal in such cases is not general deterrence, but

86

apprehension. Such offenses tend to involve victims or witnesses who can report an incident, rather than being so defined only as a result of arrest actions, as is the case with consensual crimes. Analyzing the consequences of undercover work is easier with the former type of operation than with work directed against a more general suspect group, in which deterrence is also a goal.

The case for the newer forms of undercover work, such as stings and decoys, rests on a number of inadequately tested assumptions, a fact that is ignored in the public relations efforts of advocates of these tactics, as well as by the media, which appear infatuated with the new investigative techniques. They are heralded as tactics that finally work in the war against crime, and as the only way to deal with conspirators. The dramatic effect of suddenly making a large number of arrests and recovering substantial amounts of property is stressed. But far less attention is given to other questions. What happens to crime rates during and after the operation? Who is being arrested? How does the number of arrests made or amount of property recovered compare with the accomplishments that would be expected over the same period using conventional methods? What is the cost per arrest or value of property recovered as compared with the gains under conventional methods? Any assessment of costs must include the sometimes long waiting periods aimed at establishing credibility and undercover efforts that had to be closed down because of leaks. An operation shut down because its cover is blown is far less likely to receive media attention than is one stopped after a large number of arrests. High vulnerability to discovery is an additional cost.

The research evidence on anticrime decoys and fencing stings is limited and not very reassuring. An analysis of New York City's much heralded Street Crime Unit (which specializes in decoy operations), while laudatory of the group's arrest and conviction record, did not find that the unit was ". . . decreasing either robberies or grand larcenies from a person."[31] Nor did a careful analysis of Birmingham's experiment with an antirobbery unit, which relied heavily on decoys, find it to have any effect on rates of larceny or robbery.[32]

A 1979 Justice Department study, entitled *What Happened*, makes rather grandiose claims for the success of 62 antifencing sting operations carried out since 1974.[33] But in a reanalysis, Klockars casts serious doubt on the quality of these data and their interpretation. Klockars concludes that there is no sound statistical evidence to suggest that the sting operations produced a decline in the rate of property crime.[34] An analysis of the use of federal funds for antifencing projects in San Diego over a five-year period concluded that neither the market for stolen property nor the incidence of property crimes had been reduced.[35] Walsh notes that police engaged in antifencing operations were positive in their reactions to the experience, but had ". . . serious questions as to what had really been accomplished."[36]

In general, the stings do not result in the arrest of minors because of concern over civil liability and fear of a bad press (i.e., agents are contributing to the delinquency of minors, or are leading unwary innocents into crime). Yet this age group is disproportionately responsible for property crime. Nationally, slightly over half those arrested for burglary are 17 and under,[37] yet, in the stings studied, only 3 percent of those arrested were 17 or under.

If we view the relation between police and criminals (especially those who are highly skilled) not as a war that is ultimately to be won, but as a continuing struggle with each side reciprocally responding to the other's temporary tactical advantage, then a diminishing returns effect is likely to be present. While the costs and risks of the illegality may be increased, committed criminals may simply become more clever. They are likely to make increased use of antibugging devices and engage in more sophisticated investigations and testing of potential co-conspirators.

Although the arrest of street criminals is an appropriate goal, it is important to determine what proportion of such persons are arrested. Seasoned observers note that some street criminals are adept at identifying decoys. Some of those arrested are derelicts or poverty-stricken persons in great need, or children, who cannot resist the temptation of what seems to be easy money, rather than regular street criminals. In a New York City study one in four, and in Birmingham four in ten, of those arrested through decoy operations had no previous arrest record.[38] Of course nonarrest may attest to a person's cleverness rather than purity of character. But given the transparent quality of, and publicity around, exposed wallet decoy operations, what is most striking about those who are arrested is their lack of competence. It thus seems unlikely that a large proportion of such first-time arrestees are criminals skilled in avoiding arrest. What ratio of criminals to noncriminals, or derelicts, arrested in such operations justifies a conclusion that the tactic is appropriate?

Awareness of the above can lead to a revised set of questions about the effects of undercover work. That is, are there conditions under which undercover work may cause crimes that would not have otherwise occurred? There are many individual examples of this, although evidence in the aggregate is lacking. Among the ways in which undercover work may cause or contribute to crime (at least for the particular offense in question and in the short run) are the following:

> It may generate a market for the purchase or sale of illegal goods and services and the indirect generation of capital for other illegality.
>
> It may generate the idea for the crime, for example, vice and bribery operations that involve unwary innocents.
>
> It may generate a motive. In political cases, for example, agents provocateurs may question the commitment or courage of those they seek to goad into illegal actions or may greatly encourage hostile actions which increase intramovement conflict.
>
> It may provide a missing resource, such as chemicals for drug manufacturing or plates for counterfeiting, a resource essential for the commission of the crime. Or it may offer a seductive temptation to a person who would be unlikely to encounter such temptations were it not for police actions.
>
> It may entail coercion or intimidation of a person otherwise not predisposed to commit the offense.
>
> It may generate a covert opportunity structure for illegal actions on the part of the undercover agent or informant.
>
> It may lead to retaliatory violence against informers.
>
> It may stimulate a variety of crimes on the part of those who are not targets of the undercover operation (e.g., impersonation of a police officer, crimes committed against undercover officers).

Highly complex questions with difficult measurement problems are involved here, and they pose a severe task for research. However, there is a need to ask hard questions about these operations. If claims about the effectiveness and benefits of the operations are to be accepted, the Justice Department must go much farther in permitting research by disinterested outside evaluators. Such research should be concurrent with the investigation, and not restricted to evaluations done six months after its close.

Of course, undercover operations and the behavior within them are not all of one kind. Efforts to prevent versus efforts to facilitate a crime raise different sets of issues. Having an undercover agent attempt to purchase illegal goods and services involves questions different from those related to agents' attempts at the sale of such goods and services. In general, problems appear more likely as we move from operations undertaken in response to crimes that have already occurred, or are occurring, to those that anticipate crimes that might occur. Among the latter, providing a target for victimization, as with the decoy squads, tends to raise fewer problems than do co-conspiratorial operations where the undercover agent is a willing participant in the offense. Undercover investigations which increase the opportunity for self-selection and are organized on the basis of prior intelligence or complaints, and stay close to real-world criminal conditions, seem superior to random integrity testing, or the creation of a highly artificial criminal environment with unrealistically attractive temptations.

Broad Changes in Social Control

Whatever the variations among undercover operations with respect to their legal and ethical implications, or short-term effects, actions such as ABSCAM and police-run fencing operations may be portents of a subtle and perhaps irreversible change in how social control in our society is carried out. It is well to reflect on whether this is the direction in which we wish to see our society move. It was roughly half a century ago that Secretary of War Henry Stimpson indignantly observed, in response to proposed changes in national security practices, "Gentlemen do not read each other's mail." His observation seems touchingly quaint in light of the invasions of privacy and the institution of routine surveillance that subsequent decades have witnessed. How far we have come in such a short time.

90

Fifty years from now will observers find our wondering about the propriety of attempts by police agents to bribe congressmen, distribute pornographic film, and run fencing operations equally quaint?

Broad changes in the nature of American social control appear to be taking place. We are experiencing a general shift away from some of the ideas central to the Anglo-American police tradition. The modern English police system, which Robert Peel established in 1829, worked to prevent crime by a uniformed, visible, 24-hour presence. As societal conditions have changed and as the deterrent effect of this visible and predictable police presence has been questioned, an alternative conception has gradually emerged.

Rather than only trying to decrease the opportunity for crime through a uniformed police presence, or through more recent "target hardening" approaches that increase physical security and educate citizens in crime prevention, authorities now seek to *increase* selectively the opportunity structures for crime ("target weakening"), operating under controlled conditions with nonuniformed police. Anticipatory police strategies have become more prominent.

In this respect, police strategies may be paralleling those of the modern corporation, which seeks not only to anticipate demand through market research, but also to develop and manage that demand through advertising, solicitation, and more covert types of intervention. By secretly gathering information and facilitating crime under controlled conditions, the police obtain a degree of control over the "demand" for police services hardly possible with traditional reactive practices.

Whenever a market is created rather than being a response to citizen demand, there are particular dangers of exploitation and misuse. This is as true for consumer goods as it is for criminal justice processing. Some of the "demand" for undercover police practices may be spurious. In legal systems in which authorities respond to citizen complaints rather than independently generating cases, liberty is likely more secure. There is a danger that once undercover resources are provided and skills are developed, the tactics will be used indiscriminately.

Where there is a well-documented pattern of prior infraction, the use of undercover tactics may be appropriate. Yet, given pressures on police to produce, and the power of such tactics, it is an easy move from targeted to indiscriminate use of integrity tests, and from investigation to instigation.

The bureaucratic imperative for intelligence can easily lead to the seductions of counterintelligence. On this relationship, former FBI executive William Sullivan observed, "As far as I'm concerned, we might as well not engage in intelligence activities without counterintelligence. One is the right arm, the other the left. They work together."[39]

The allure and the power of undercover tactics may make them irresistible. Just as most societies that have discovered alcohol have seen its use spread, once undercover tactics become legitimate and resources are available for them, they are likely to spread to new areas and be put to questionable use. To some observers the use of questionable or bad undercover means is nevertheless justified because it serves good ends. Who, after all, cannot be indignant over violations of the public trust on the part of those sworn to uphold it, or the hidden taxes we all pay because of organized crime? One of the problems with such arguments is, of course, that there is no guarantee that bad means will be restricted to good ends.

An important party to the elaboration and diffusion of undercover tactics is likely to be police trained in governmental programs, who may face mandatory retirement at age 55 if they are not attracted to the more lucrative private sector long before that. The police lieutenant who was the central figure in the widely publicized stings in Washington, D.C., retired and opened his own securities investigation firm — "Sting Security, Inc." — and Mel Weinberg has started his own private investigation agency, called "Abscam Incorporated."[40] Perhaps we will reach the point where some type of registration will be needed for former government agents trained and experienced in highly "sensitive" operations who continue such work in private enterprise. The case of the former CIA agents working for Libya could easily have its domestic counterparts.

From current practices, we may not be far from activities such as the following. Rather than infiltrating criminal enterprises or starting up their own sham enterprises, police agents (such as accounting specialists) might infiltrate legitimate businesses to be sure they are obeying the law, or to ensure that they would obey it if given a government-engendered chance not to. The IRS might secretly sponsor a promotion sweepstakes and then prosecute those who fail to report their winnings accurately. Following a wonderful Don Quixote tale, husbands or wives, or those considering marriage, might hire attractive members of the opposite sex to test their partner's fidelity. Businesses might create false fronts using undercover agents to involve their competitors in illegal actions for which they would then be arrested. A business could be sabotaged through infiltration by disruptive workers, or its public image could be damaged by a rival's taking false front actions in its name.

In the case of ABSCAM, we have the irony of Congress giving the FBI funds for undercover activities that were then used to finance actions against Congress. With Watergate not yet a decade past, one can imagine a more sinister reciprocal pattern. This would involve using some of the money and undercover dirty tricks to help elect friendly congressmen, who would then increase the appropriation, generating an endless cycle.

The deterrence sought through the use of undercover tactics comes, in the words of an experienced undercover agent, through "[creating] in the minds of potential offenders an apprehension that any 'civilian' could, in fact, be a police officer." Whether this tactic deters or merely makes sophisticated criminals more clever, while also encouraging new crimes on the part of the weak and the gullible, is a question for research. One can also ask what is the effect of ever more sophisticated ruses and elaborate surveillance on trust among law-abiding citizens? To many observers, American society is fragmented enough without the government's adding a new layer of suspiciousness and distrust. It is possible that, the greater the public's knowledge of such tactics, the greater the mutual distrust among American citizens.

In recent decades, undercover police activities such as COINTEL and the many local varieties damaged the protected freedoms of political dissenters. But now, through a spill-over effect, they may be inhibiting the speech of a much broader segment of society. The free and open speech protected by the Bill of Rights may be chilled for everyone. After ABSCAM, for example, people in government cannot help but wonder who it is they are dealing with. Communication may become more guarded and the free and open dialogue traditionally seen as necessary in high levels of government inhibited. Similar effects may occur in business and private life.

A major demand in totalitarian countries that undergo liberalization is for the abolition of the secret police and secret police tactics. Fake documents, lies, subterfuge, infiltration, secret and intrusive surveillance, and the creation of apparent reality are not generally associated with United States law enforcement. However, we may be taking small but steady steps toward the paranoia and suspicion that characterize many totalitarian countries. Even if unfounded, once such feelings are aroused and become part of the culture, they are not easily dissipated.

Soothsayers of doom are likely to become increasingly apparent as we approach 1984. The cry of "wolf" is easy to utter and hence easy to dismiss. Liberty is a complex condition, and under democratic government there are forces and counterforces serving both to jeopardize and protect that condition. That is, tactics that threaten liberties can also be used to protect them. However, neither complexity, sophistry, nor the need for prudence in sounding alarms should blind us from seeing the implications of recent undercover work for the redefinition and extension of government control. Lewis, in *It Can't Happen Here*, argues that if totalitarianism comes to America, it will be in traditional American form.[41] It will be by accretion and the gradual erosion of traditional liberties, rather than by cataclysmic changes. The issues raised by recent police undercover actions go far beyond whether a given representative was predisposed to take a bribe or the development of effective guidelines.

Such police actions are part of a process of the rationalization of crime control that began in the nineteenth century. Social control has gradually become more specialized and technical, and, in some ways, more penetrating and intrusive. The state's power to punish and to gather information has been extended deeper into the social fabric, although not necessarily in a violent way. We are seeing a shift in social control from direct coercion used after the fact to anticipatory actions entailing deception, manipulation, and planning. New technocratic agents of social control are replacing the rough-and-ready cowboys of an earlier era. They are part of what Foucault refers to as the modern state's "subtle calculated technology of subjection."[42]

Here, undercover practices take their place beside varied technological advances:

New or improved data-gathering techniques, such as lasers, parabolic mikes and other bugs, wiretaps, videotaping and still photography, remote camera systems, periscopic prisms, one-way mirrors, various infrared, sensor, and tracking devices, truth serum, polygraphs, voice print and stress analysis, pen registers, ultraviolet radiation, and helicopter and satellite surveillance.

New data-processing techniques based on silicone computer chips, which enable inexpensive storing, retrieval, and analysis of personal information that previously was not collected—or, if collected, not kept; or, if kept, not capable of being brought together inexpensively in seconds. To this must be added the increased prominence of computers (with their attendant records) in everyday affairs, whether involving commerce, banking, telephones, medicine, education, employment, criminal justice, pay television, or even library transactions.

An increase in the amount and variety of data available as a result of new reporting requirements (e.g., at one extreme, the pressure for some form of a national identification system), and an increase in private entrepreneurs who collect and disseminate personal data.

The vast and continuing expansion of the private security industry (which is, according to some estimates, now three times the size of the public police force). This is staffed by thousands of former military, national security, and domestic police agents schooled and experienced in the latest control techniques while working for the government, but now much less subject to its control.

Increasing centralization, standardization, and integration of law enforcement agencies (e.g., regionalization and merger plans at the local level; the absorption of the Alcohol, Firearms and Tobacco Agency into the Secret Service and suggestions to add the Drug Enforcement Agency to the FBI at the federal level; joint local-state-federal enforcement efforts; a new domestic role for the CIA; and standardized operating procedures inspired by new Justice Department funding efforts).

Evolving techniques of behavior modification, manipulation, and control, including operant conditioning, pharmacology, genetic engineering, psychosurgery, and subliminal communication.

Taken in isolation and with appropriate safeguards, each of these technological advances may have appropriate uses and justifications. However, the techniques become more problematic when seen in consort and as part of an emerging trend. Observers will differ as to whether they see in this an emerging totalitarian fortress, or benign tools for a society ravaged by crime and disorder. But regardless of how the trend is seen, it is clear that some of our traditional notions of social control are undergoing profound change. There is a need for careful analysis and public discussion of the complex issues involved.

NOTES

1. See, e.g., Sam Sieber, *Fatal Remedies* (New York: Plenum, 1981).
2. The discussion here continues my interest in covert forms of interdependence between rule breakers and enforcers. See also the following: "Thoughts on a Neglected Category of Social Movement Participant: Agents Provocateurs and Informants," *American Journal of Sociology,* September 1974, pp. 402–42; "Double Agents," *New Republic,* Oct. 18, 1975, pp. 8–13; "External Efforts to Damage or Facilitate Social Movements," in *The Dynamics of Social Movements,* Mayer Zald and John McCarthy, eds. (Cambridge, Mass.: Winthrop, 1979), pp. 94–125; "The New Police Undercover Work," *Urban Life and Culture,* January 1980, pp. 400–46; "Ironies of Social Control: Authorities as Contributors to Deviance through Escalation, Non-Enforcement, and Covert Facilitation," *Social Problems,* February 1981, pp. 221–46; "Types of Undercover Operation and Activities" (Paper delivered at Hastings Center Conference on Undercover Activities, Hastings-on-Hudson, N.Y., 1981); "Undercover Police Tactics," *Encyclopedia of Crime and Justice,* forthcoming.
3. *Hoffa* v. *U.S.,* 385 U.S. 293 (1963); *Lewis* v. *U.S.,* 385 U.S. 323 (1966); *Osborn* v. *U.S.,* 385 U.S. 323 (1966); *U.S.* v. *Russell,* 411 U.S. 423 (1973); *Hampton* v. *U.S.,* 425 U.S. 484 (1976); *U.S.* v. *Twigg,* 588 F. 2d 373 (3rd Cir. 1978).
4. John Fullam, "Memorandum and Order," U.S. District Court for the Eastern District of Pennsylvania, *U.S.* v. *Harry P. Jannotte, George Schwartz,* no. 80–166, November 1980.
5. *Newsweek,* Nov. 15, 1976.
6. Nat Hentoff, *Village Voice,* Dec. 31, 1980. In a useful series of articles from November to January, Hentoff gives forceful consideration to the civil liberties issues raised by ABSCAM. In general, these issues have received only cursory attention in the media.
7. Fullam, "Memorandum and Order."
8. *Los Angeles Times,* Nov. 17, 1977.
9. *Newsweek,* Nov. 15, 1976; John Lardner, "How Prosecutors Are Nabbed," *New Republic,* Jan. 29, 1977, pp. 22–25.
10. *Sherman* v. *U.S.,* 356 U.S. 369, 372 (1974).
11. J. Edgar Hoover, with his files on important people, was a master at the use of this technique. Watergate has been interpreted as an effort to gather data for blackmail and political leverage rather than for publication. In a shocking example, Southern Bell Company executives used wiretap material in an effort to coerce local officials into agreeing to rate increases (George O'Toole, *The Private Sector: Rent-a-Cops, Private Spies and*

the Police-Industrial Complex [New York: W.W. Norton, 1978], p. 70). As the main "head-hunter" of the Internal Affairs Unit, and later as chief of police, William Parker is said to have used such tactics to control the Los Angeles Police Department and its broader political environment. The myth of secret knowledge can be a powerful control factor spreading fear among those who have things to hide. Rumors of the secret information Parker supposedly had worked to his advantage. Joseph Woods ("The Progressives and the Police: Urban Reform and the Professionalization of the Los Angeles Police" [Ph.D. diss., University of California at Los Angeles, 1973], p. 420) observes, "Newspaper reports implied that Parker knew dreadful things about one or another public figure, and that his secret files made him and the Department invulnerable to political interference." Within bureaucracies such as the police, holding in abeyance negative information that can always be used against a person is a major (and unstudied) form of internal control. One police officer notes, "It was like being in a game where the umpires had two rule books and wouldn't tell you which one you were playing under" (Sonny Grosso and Philip Rosenberg, *Point Blank* [New York: Avon, 1979], p. 189).

12. *New York Times,* May 17, 1979.
13. Kurt Vonnegut, *Mother-Night* (New York: Dell, 1975).
14. Lawrence Linderman, "Underground Angel," *Playboy,* July 1981, pp. 134–36, 142, 220–235, 244.
15. *Chicago Daily News,* Sept. 24, 1975.
16. *Boston Globe,* Oct. 26, 1979.
17. See, e.g., Peter K. Manning and Laurence Redlinger, "Invitational Edges of Corruption: Some Consequences of Narcotics Law Enforcement," in *Politics and Drugs,* Paul Rock, ed. (New York: E. P. Dutton/Society Books, 1977), pp. 279–310; Robert Daley, *Prince of the City* (Boston: Little, Brown, 1978).
18. Whited, *Chiodo* (Chicago: Playboy Press, 1974).
19. *New York Times,* July 30, 1978.
20. Fullam, "Memorandum and Order"; Irving Nathan, "ABSCAM—Production of Supplemental Information to Defense Counsel" (memorandum: Washington, D.C.: Justice Department, Jan. 6, 1981); Stephen Kaufman and Daniel Rezneck, "Post-Hearing Memorandum in Support of Defendant Frank Thompson, Jr.'s Motion to Dismiss the Indictment on Due Process Grounds," March 1980, *U.S.* v. *Frank Thompson, Jr. et al.,* no. CR-80-00291 (Pratt, J.); *Boston Globe,* July 18, 1980. In the classic fashion of the double agent, some of Weinberg's compensation appears to have come from his deceiving the government, beyond the intended targets of the deception. He was paid a $15,000 reward for helping to recover $2 billion worth of supposedly stolen certificates of deposit. However, there is evidence to suggest that the certificates were counterfeit and were never actually stolen, but rather were created under Weinberg's tutelage. He then "recovered" them for the reward money (Jack Anderson, United Features Syndicate, May 28, 1981).
21. Nick Kotz, "ABSCAM's Loose Cannons," *New Republic,* Mar. 29, 1980, pp. 21–25, citing the account of *Newsday* correspondent Anthony Marro.
22. *New York Times,* May 18, 1979. Another potential hidden cost in undercover operations involves the goods or money that is exchanged. In a Seattle case a judge ruled that patrons of a bar who purchased color televisions and stereos from undercover agents did not have to return them. The goods were not actually stolen, but purchased by police through an LEAA grant. The status of the nearly $500,000 which the government paid out in nine ABSCAM cases is less clear; only $50,000 had been recovered by the end of

1981 (*New York Times,* Sept. 18, 1981). In a related vein is the dispute over what should happen to a $5,000 bribe paid by an FBI operative as part of a "staged crime" to the police superintendent of Bridgeport, Connecticut. The superintendent arrested the former convict bearing the bribe and took possession of the FBI's bugging equipment. Moments later FBI agents appeared and unsuccessfully sought the release of the operative and return of the equipment and money. The mayor of Bridgeport ordered that the $5,000 be spent to buy Christmas toys for poor children, while the FBI continued to demand that the money be returned (*New York Times,* Aug. 21, 1981).

23. *New York Times,* June 4, 1980.

24. Fred Graham, *The Alias Program* (Boston: Little, Brown, 1977). See also the poignant case of Tom Leonhardt. His former wife, their two children, and her new husband, a criminal witness, were relocated by the Witness Protection Program. Leonhardt spent eight difficult years trying to find his children. The story is told in Leslin Waller's *Hide in Plain Sight* (New York: Dell, 1980) and in a film of the same title.

25. *National Law Journal,* Oct. 20, 1980. Of course, it is also possible to argue that third parties may be saved from victimization because such undercover work prevents crime that would have occurred in its absence. This may be through deterrence or incapacitation (e.g., some unknown proportion of persons may be saved from victimization while those arrested through a sting are in jail). But cases as the one in Colorado have a reality and poignancy that make it hard to give equivalent attention to this argument.

26. Department of Justice, *What Happened* (Washington, D.C.: U.S. Government Printing Office, 1979), p. 4. Even were documentation presented, a high rate of return might simply be an artifact of the method. For example, undercover agents may be encouraged to purchase only easily identifiable stolen goods that can be returned to their owner. Adequate understanding of the effect of government fences on victimized persons requires knowing (1) what percentage of property brought to a government fence by a thief is stolen in the expectation that it will be purchased by the fence, (2) what percentage of this property is actually purchased by the fence, and (3) what percentage of the goods that are purchased is returned? The first question presents the most difficult measurement issues. Yet in many cases it seems clear that the theft is undertaken with a government fence in mind. For example, an El Paso, Texas, fencing sting conducted by local police and the United States Customs Agency set up in a storefront called JRE Apartment Complex Maintenance and Repair Shop. In the year the sting was in operation almost $2 million in stolen property was purchased. A major contributor to this was a man and his girl friend who, over a five-month period, sold the project seventeen stolen automobiles, four trucking rigs with five semitrailers, and two trailer loads of merchandise. The total recovery value of the items purchased from this couple was put at $575,909 (Catherine Cotter and James Burrows, *Property Crime Program: A Special Report: Overview of the Sting Program and Project Summaries* [Washington, D.C.: Justice Department, January 1981]). Making such a large number of purchases from the same persons over a period of time certainly seems questionable policy. Issues related to how long an operation should go on, how many buys should be made from a person after sufficient evidence for prosecution has been obtained, and how many times a target should be approached after initially refusing an illegal offer have received little policy attention, particularly at the local level. Most departments have no guidelines for the conduct of undercover activities.

27. *New York Times,* May 18, 1979.

28. Cyril Payne, *Deep Cover* (New York: Newsweek, 1979).

29. Four Philadelphia police officers from a decoy squad were recently indicted by a federal grand jury on the grounds that they had framed eight suspects on robbery charges. In one of these cases two suspects claimed they were arrested as they bent over to help the decoy pick up a roll of bills he had dropped. The police were members of an aggressive squad whose arrest totals easily exceeded those of other decoy squads working in the central business district (*New York Times,* Sept. 13, 1981).

30. *New York Post,* Mar. 29, 1978.

31. Abt Associates, *New York City Anti-Crime Patrol—Exemplary Project Validation Report* (Washington, D.C.: National Institute of Law Enforcement and Criminal Justice, 1974).

32. Mary Ann Wycoff, Charles Brown, and Robert Petersen, *Birmingham Anti-Robbery Unit Evaluation Report* (Washington, D.C.: Police Foundation, 1980).

33. Dept. of Justice, *What Happened.*

34. Carl Klockars, "Jonathan Wilde and the Modern Sting," in *History and Crime: Implications for Criminal Justice Policy,* James A. Inciardi and Charles E. Taupel (Beverly Hills, Calif.: Sage, 1980).

35. Susan Pennell, "Fencing Activity and Police Strategy," *Police Chief,* September 1979, pp. 71–75.

36. Mary Walsh, *Strategies for Combatting the Criminal Receiver of Stolen Goods* (Washington, D.C.: Law Enforcement Assistance Administration, 1975), p. 114.

37. Federal Bureau of Investigation, *Uniform Crime Reports* (Washington, D.C.: U.S. Government Printing Office, 1977), p. 174.

38. New York City Police Department, "Survey of Criminal Records of Perpetrators Arrested by Members of the Street Crime Unit" (memorandum; Apr. 5, 1974); Wycoff, Brown, and Petersen, *Birmingham Anti-Robbery Unit Evaluation.*

39. William Sullivan, *The Bureau: My Thirty Years in Hoover's FBI* (New York: W.W. Norton, 1979), p. 128.

40. Charles Conconi and Toni House, *The Washington Sting* (New York: Coward, McCann & Geoghegan, 1979); *Newsweek,* Oct. 26, 1981. Of course, undercover tactics are certainly not new to the private sector. Indeed, such tactics were largely brought to federal police agencies from the private sector through persons such as Alan Pinkerton and William J. Burns.

41. Sinclair Lewis, *It Can't Happen Here* (New York: American Library, 1973).

42. Michel Foucault, *Discipline and Punish: The Birth of the Prison* (New York: Pantheon, 1977).

5

Licensing Criminals: Police and Informants

Peter Reuter*

THE POLICE HAVE ALWAYS HAD effective discretion in administering the law. That is, they have been forced, by limitations in resources as well as by political concerns, to make choices about which offenses will generate action on their part. In the last 15 years,[1] there has come to be a public recognition of the need for police discretion and an understanding of its complex consequences. This in turn has led to occasional demands for articulation of formal guidelines for lower level officers—who actually

* The views expressed here are solely the responsibility of the author and should not be identified with those of Rand or its sponsors. Lisa Rodriguez provided helpful research assistance.

exercise the discretion—to follow.[2] Police executives have been notably and understandably reluctant to provide such formal guidelines.

Their reluctance is understandable because there is in fact no basis in law for their use of discretion. Goldstein (1960) has shown that the statutes of the various states make no provision for the police to decide which violations are worthy of action and which should be ignored.[3] They must, by law, act against all statutory violations. It is clear that they do not and that, if they are to function effectively, they cannot. The formal statement of guidelines stating, for example, that possession of less than one ounce of marijuana is not grounds for arrest involves challenge to the legislature and courts.[4] Yet, without guidelines, the police must always remain subject to the charge of selective and discriminatory enforcement.[5]

The problem becomes particularly acute in police dealings with informants. The public has certain expectations of police performance that can be met only if the police enter into long-term cooperative relationships with criminals. For example, drug dealers who invest a great deal of effort in insulating themselves from dealings with strangers often can be apprehended only if the police enlist the assistance of their confederates. Similarly, the demand that the police solve major cases promptly requires that they be able to tap into the network of information held by criminals. In order to carry out these tasks, as well as some others, the police must issue what in effect are licenses to certain criminals. We may protest that when we allowed that the police must have discretion, we did not propose that they enter into the business of licensing criminals. Nonetheless, that is merely discretion writ large.

The licensing process is not one which agencies are readily able to control. Police and informants both mistrust any effort to formalize the relationship and to require recording of their transactions. The informant is concerned with possible betrayal while the officer does not want to lose control of the information. Efforts to formalize and control will lead either to evasion or less effective policing.

Police agencies cannot devise usable guidelines to cover the kinds of licenses that the police may offer informants. Such guidelines not only would directly flout the legislative process but either they must be at so high a level of generality as to be of no help to the individual officer or they will fail to command consensus. Either we must accept the tensions created by the ill-monitored licensing or we must lower our demands upon the police to apprehend certain classes of criminals.

The term police is used here to cover criminal investigative agencies generally. In particular, the FBI and the Drug Enforcement Administration (DEA) will provide much of the illustrative material. The demands placed on these agencies force them into the licensing process, while their general stature enables them to offer more effective protection for their licensees.

Criminal Licenses: Some Examples

There exists a small, rather distinguished, academic literature on police-informant dealings. The three major studies all deny that police agencies do in fact issue broad licenses. While acknowledging that the best informants are not those who work for money but rather those who are "working off" charges, each writer claims that the police he studied do not knowingly overlook the criminal activities of their informants, except where it falls outside their investigative interest.

Skolnick (1966) dealt with relations between detectives and informants in a western city. He noted that detective squads were narrowly concerned with specific activities and would ignore other activities of their informants. Narcotics detectives overlooked thefts by their informants, while the robbery squad would ignore narcotics use by its informants.[6] Nonetheless, he argued that the police offered only the most restrictive licenses to their informants; anytime a police officer could obtain hard evidence against an informant he would use it to increase the pressure on the informant to help make additional cases.

Manning (1980) also reported on narcotic unit relations with informants. He observed that, although informants were expected to continue drug use (why otherwise would they be able to provide information about drug dealers?), they were not permitted to act as dealers. "A final indication that the snitch (informant) may be manipulating an agent is evidence that he may be dealing drugs while working for the police department. This means that he is using his status as an informant to carry on a business and that he may be informing to the police to reduce his competition."[7]

The third major study is Wilson's (1978), which is the only detailed account of federal agencies' dealings with informants. This description of the FBI and DEA is consistent with Manning's: Informants are most useful when they are providing information in exchange for reduced charges, but the DEA and FBI do not admit to permitting their informants to continue criminal dealings. Indeed, in 1976, following the revelations of COINTELPRO,[8] the attorney general promulgated strict guidelines on informants' behavior. "Informants are not to commit acts of violence, use unlawful methods to gain information, initiate a plan to commit a criminal act or participate in a criminal act except insofar as the FBI determines that such participation is necessary to obtain information needed for the purposes of a federal prosecution."[9] Nonetheless, Wilson notes that there is some allowance for the use of discretion, particularly with respect to the seriousness of the informant's violation.

Each of these studies is based on extensive fieldwork. Manning and Skolnick spent months as participant-observers in the detective units they studied. Wilson had access to numerous files in FBI and DEA field offices and spent many hours in unstructured interviews with agents in those offices. These claims about the restrictions on informants are not to be treated lightly.

Nonetheless, once one moves away from the scholarly literature, which is police-focused, a very different picture emerges. There are credible accounts of honest police agents providing quite broad licenses to their regular informants, as well as materials filed in court proceedings that strongly suggest licensing.

In the course of a study of illegal markets in New York (Reuter, 1983), I had regular contact with an informant. Joe was a bookmaker with almost 20 years of experience. He had been imprisoned once and arrested numerous times. For some time, he had run an undercover bookmaking operation for a local law enforcement agency, after the agency had arrested him and convinced him that he was likely to go to prison if he did not cooperate. During the period that he ran the bookmaking operation under surveillance, he had earned a considerable sum, probably more than $100,000 in a year; the operation had led to the arrest and conviction of perhaps a dozen bookmakers and their associates.

At the time I had dealings with Joe, the undercover operation had ended and Joe had gone back into the bookmaking business on his own, working with a number of the better-known bookmakers in New York. He continued to provide information to a number of law enforcement agencies, both federal and local.

During the period of our contact, Joe was arrested at least three times on bookmaking charges. The third time he was arrested by an agency he had never dealt with in a jurisdiction where prosecutors and judges were known to be tough on gambling offenses. He asked his contacts in various other agencies to intercede for him, which they did, with the result that he was placed on probation. At least two of the agencies who called on his behalf knew of his dealings in the bookmaking business at that time. Indeed, one of them, according to Joe, had initially approached him by saying that they had no interest in his own bookmaking but wanted to get information about the people with whom he dealt.

Vilano (1977) provides some interesting details about his dealings with criminal informants during a 20-year career as an FBI agent specializing in organized crime investigations in New York. Vilano describes himself as particularly successful in recruiting Mafia members as informants. In most cases, the informants were embittered and unsuccessful; nonetheless, while under Vilano's supervision, they participated in a variety of activities which many of us would take as fairly serious criminal offenses. "Of my first three member sources, only Micky Flowers continued to be an active criminal. Jackie Gucci stuck to a genteel kind of loansharking, while Rico Conte limited his muscle to pushing around vending machines."[10] Clearly, agent attitudes are relaxed about criminal activities. At another stage, Vilano placed a bet with a bookmaker through one of his informants, simply because he didn't have access to a bookmaker himself."[11]

Vilano is also explicit about the moral dilemma presented by licensing informants. "The most troublesome aspect . . . was the worry that I handed out a license to steal. Billeti [an informant] realized how valuable he was to me, and he knew I would try to protect him if he was caught. I had to take the position of never wanting to know anything that he was going to do ahead of time unless it was for the benefit of the Bureau."[12] "I knew that I was perpetuating the career of a criminal, but I believed that the information Billeti gave us was worth much more than what he managed to steal."[13]

Less explicit, but quite compelling, evidence is provided in documents routinely filed in court proceedings. Consider, for example, the following description of an informant taken from a wiretap application by the FBI in Kansas City.[14]

> Confidential Informant Number 10 (CI #10) has provided agents of the FBI with information on a confidential basis in excess of six years, which information has proven reliable based upon reports of other confidential informants and by independent investigation. CI #10 has furnished information in approximately 15 investigations, such information and other information having been obtained through personal contact, conversation with and observation of conversations between numerous individuals involved with the Kansas City 'Outfit.'

It is hardly plausible that this describes anyone other than a member or close associate of the "Outfit" (the Kansas City term for Mafia) involved in their activities in a fairly substantial way. Such descriptions of informants, varying somewhat in explicitness, often appear in wiretap applications.

We should note also the existence of an FBI informant effort called the Top Echelon program. This program, whose existence was not acknowledged for some years,[15] consists of efforts to recruit high-level members of organized crime, mostly the Mafia, to provide information on a regular basis. Probably "CI #10" referred to in the wiretap quotation is a Top Echelon informant. But is is certainly implausible that the TE's, as they are called, engage in criminal activities only for the purposes of providing information to the FBI. More plausibly, they gain a certain amount of protection in return for the information, much of which they may use for strategic advantage, informing against their rivals within the family.

The potential licensing powers of the FBI are unique for at least two reasons. First, its prestige enables it to coerce local agencies into protection of FBI informants without offering reciprocal service. Indeed, the standard complaint in many local agencies is precisely that the FBI always demands and never reciprocates. The FBI's long-cherished belief in its own integrity and the probable corruption of all other law enforcement agencies provides its rationale for this behavior.[16] Whatever the reason, the result is that the FBI is better able to protect any informants it chooses to license than are other agencies.[17]

More fundamental, though, is the difference in investigative focus. Local agencies devote most of their resources to activities other than the solving of crimes or the control of illegal markets. Patrol activities, the processing of arrests, community relations, etc., take up most of their time. Even when dealing with organized crime and with drug markets, the local agencies are likely to focus their efforts on the lowest and most visible level of activity. They simply have less need for the kind of informant who must be given a long leash in order to provide information that the agency needs to make the desired kinds of cases. Certainly one explanation for the findings of Manning and Skolnick concerning the narcotics units they observed is that these units simply did not try to make cases much above the retail level.[18]

One local unit that did attempt to make more ambitious cases was the Special Investigations Unit (SIU) of the New York Police Department. The SIU's mission was to make major conspiracy cases against heroin and cocaine dealers in the city which was seen as the national center for these groups. Its members were given great freedom from supervision and made many spectacular cases, as recounted in Daley (1978). However, it also turned out to be an extremely corrupt unit, whose members made substantial sums of money at the same time as they were making successful cases against major dealers.

The central figure in revealing the corruption of the SIU was Robert Leuci, one of the more successful members of the unit. Exemplifying the problem of making cases in this area were his relationships with his best informant, the Baron. "About twice a year the Baron gets arrested by other [narcotics] teams. Each time Leuci rushes to court, speaks to the district attorney and judge, the Baron gets out on parole they go back to work."[19] What is interesting here is the ease with which Leuci was apparently able to obtain the Baron's release. The Baron was not a major dealer, but certainly sold at least one or usually two steps above the retail level in the market. Yet Leuci was able to get his release on a number of occasions, though dealing with different agencies. Corruption of these agencies was not necessary; such transactions were apparently commonplace.

The Necessity of Licenses

It is no mystery why the police become issuers of criminal licenses. The adage "to catch a thief, use a thief" summarizes it straightforwardly enough. Detective novels notwithstanding, it is difficult for the police to solve many cases without the cooperation of criminal colleagues of the person who committed it. The agencies argue that they are able to obtain cooperation from criminals without condoning the informants' continued participation in criminal activities. I suggest that this is not so, that we place demands on the police which can only be satisfied if the police enter into long-term cooperative relationships with a number of criminals.

For the purposes of this discussion, it is useful to employ a distinction between two classes of police activity suggested by Wilson.[20] He distinguishes between investigation, where the police seek to obtain information leading to the arrest of a person associated with a specific crime that has already occurred, and instigation, for which the police suspect that a certain individual is involved in a continuing pattern of criminal activity and seek to place an agent (informant or undercover agent) in a position to observe a criminal act. Drug dealing provides the most significant focus of instigative activity.

Police require a coterie of active criminal informants for both purposes. Consider, as an example of investigation, a major robbery. If the perpetrators are not arrested or identified within hours of the incident, the police have small prospect of solving the case (Greenwood et al., 1975). Their most effective source of information is an immediate checking with all the informants they have in the world of thieves and fences. Those who carried out the robbery are likely to have involved other confederates in the planning or to need some assistance in disposing of its fruits. Various pieces of information about the crime are likely to be floating around the network of people involved in theft and fencing.

It is scarcely plausible that these informants consist solely of persons working off charges. The police need for information is immediate. They must have a pool of potential sources available at all times. If these sources are to be of value, they must be active criminals. They will

107

provide information in the reasonable expectation that the agency will help them when next they get into trouble. The detective who cracks a major robbery case with the help of an informant will certainly be the first person the informant calls when he is next arrested, although if it is a homicide, or other serious offense, the detective will not and cannot help.

This is not to say that the informant regularly tells the cooperating officer about all activities, to ask permission. That would serve the interest of neither, though Vilano says that one of his informants would occasionally ask advice about getting into a particular criminal deal, usually one he was hesitant about and wanted Vilano to dissuade him from. There is likely to be an informal understanding about the nature of the license and the set of activities for which the informant will get assistance when caught.

Instigation is the more complex and ambiguous activity for the police, because their own agents must get involved in the workings of the criminal world. For instigation to be effective, an introduction is necessary, and only criminal informants can provide that. Heroin enforcement is a good example because that is where the problems of this technique are most acute.

One model of heroin enforcement using informants would not require any licensing of the form I have been discussing. This is a variant of "buy and bust," in which the agent arranges to buy a certain amount of heroin from a dealer, and then arrests the dealer immediately after the sale. The dealer has the option of introducing the agent to the supplier or facing significant prison time. The undercover agent is then able to move up the chain from retail to major distributor without giving anyone a license to deal. The introduction gets the dealer out of the immediate charge, but confers no future privilege.

Undoubtedly, much narcotics enforcement operates this way. But narcotics agencies also collect intelligence. Because starting each investigation with a low-level buy and proceeding up the distribution chain is wasteful, narcotics agents must choose the targets of their enforcement based on a continuing evaluation of the significance of particular dealers. Middle-level dealers who are willing to arrange introductions to higher-level dealers on the promise of anonymity provide a far more efficient method of reaching the targeted dealer than starting on the long and uncertain chain from retail level.

Thus, instigative agencies are strongly motivated to issue licenses to informants. An ounce dealer who regularly turns in useful leads on quarter-pound dealers can expect to be left alone, and even to get help if another agency becomes interested, as long as the level of activity stays low. The extent of this licensing is a function of the level of market that the agency is aiming at. It is not surprising that the DEA, which has prime responsibility for making high-level cases, is suspected of issuing the broadest licenses.[21] Like the FBI, DEA can be extremely helpful to local agencies, which often depend on it for training and equipment as well as for information.

But there is a major difference in the relations detectives maintain with the two classes of informants. Instigative informants are likely to be much more intimately involved in the activities of the unit with which they work. They often determine the targets of the unit's enforcement efforts[22] and, because they are involved in almost daily criminal offenses, are much more likely to need the unit's intercession. In contrast, relations between other kinds of detectives and their "snitches" are much more attenuated; detectives seek the criminal's assistance for a particular case and the criminal only rarely needs to invoke the aid of the detective.

Managing the Licensing Process

It is difficult to describe how agencies manage programs whose existence they barely acknowledge. Indeed, calls to various police agencies in the Washington area yielded only one explicit set of guidelines covering agent-informant relationships, that of the FBI. DEA said that these guidelines were confidential, and two police departments (the Metropolitan Police Department of Washington, D.C., and the Montgomery County, Maryland, Police Department) said, after some initial confusion, that no such guidelines existed.

The FBI guidelines were promulgated in 1976, as part of Attorney General Edward Levi's brief effort to bring the FBI more firmly under the control of the Department of Justice.[23] The version reviewed here is a revision that went into effect in December 1980, after ABSCAM had broken. Though the guidelines refer to the problems of criminal license, they address only vaguely the extent to which such license should be limited. Extensive quotation from the relevant section of the guidelines makes the point clearly enough:

> Informants who are in a position to have useful knowledge of criminal activities often are themselves involved in a criminal livelihood. It is recognized that in the course of using an informant or confidential source, the FBI may receive limited information concerning a variety of criminal activities by the informant or confidential source and that in regard to less serious participation in criminal activities unconnected to an FBI assignment, it may be necessary to forego any further investigative or enforcement action in order to retain the source of information. However, whenever a Special Agent learns of the commission of a *serious crime* by an informant or confidential source he shall notify a field office supervisor. The supervisor shall make a determination whether to notify appropriate state or local law enforcement or prosecutive authorities of any violation of law . . .[24]
>
> In determining whether to notify appropriate state or local law enforcement or prosecutive authorities of criminal activity by FBI informants and confidential sources, the FBI shall consider:
> (a) whether the crime is completed, imminent or inchoate;
> (b) the seriousness of the crime in terms of danger to life and property; . . .[25]

Clearly, this leaves a great deal of discretion to both the individual special agent, about whether to report a particular activity of an informant to a supervisor, and to the supervisor about whether to pass this information on to any other agency. The stress on danger to life and property suggests that a great deal of latitude is intended. Certainly a bookmaker or, as Vilano put it, "genteel" loanshark, may be left undisturbed.

How is this discretion used? This, of course, is a matter about which the FBI is understandably very sensitive. Efforts by the General Accounting Office (GAO) to review the compliance of the FBI informant program with the guidelines have been notably unsuccessful. The Bureau maintained that any audit of informant files by GAO would compromise

110

the integrity of the program;[26] it is instructive that this claim has not been successfully challenged, despite GAO's intimate involvement in many sensitive areas of national security policy.

Having beaten off GAO, the FBI nonetheless felt an obligation to carry out its own audit of the program to determine compliance with the attorney general's guidelines. The FBI staff reviewed all active informant files and a sample of closed files. It declared that only a trivial number of instances of minor non-compliance were found. Those instances of non-compliance included one failure of an agent to report a criminal violation on the part of an informant. But the report is silent on the general issue of criminal violations by informants and discloses nothing about the nature of the license issued by individual agents.

Congress then asked GAO to review the FBI audit. That review, in its dry bureaucratic way, permitted the GAO to vent its ire concerning the usurpation of its own audit function. Two observations in the GAO report are of particular interest here. First, the FBI audit did not include any interviews with informants or agents. Instead, agents were asked to respond to a questionnaire, without any promise of confidentiality,[27] and the inspectors looked at what was recorded in the files. As GAO commented, "To accept file data as accurate, or to accept the lack of it as proof that everything was handled properly, assumes that agents who had deviated from FBI and Attorney General regulations would have recorded that fact in the files."[28] That does indeed seem unlikely.

The second fact of some interest is that the FBI claims to have had, in 1979, only 2,847 active informants. Considering that approximately 2,000 special agents are involved in organized crime investigations alone, and almost 3,000 more deal with white-collar crime, this seems an implausibly small number. I conjecture, that numerous informants (obviously not including ones who receive authorized payments from the Bureau) are not in fact included in the files. They may instead receive informal assistance from individual agents. The Justice Department, in commenting on this issue raised by GAO, said, "The Department believes that no reasonable audit procedures will insure the detection of improprieties, especially if collusion is involved."[29] Again this seems a reasonable assumption, if a damning one.

The FBI is not the only agency to respond to scandal by the promulgation of informant controls. The New York Police Department (NYPD) was spurred by the findings of the Knapp Commission and the revelations of corruption in their elite narcotics squad, described in Daley (1978), to formalize its informant program and to control agent dealings with criminals. Each informant must now be registered with the department and payments to the informant subject to scrutiny.

Considerable skepticism has been expressed on the efficacy of the system. Kleinman (1980) gathered a number of comments by former and current members of the NYPD. Many doubted that officers or informants had sufficient confidence in the integrity of the system to accept registration. He cited one narcotics detective as saying, "When you register someone, they clam up right away . . . The only time I'd register someone is if I had to pay him a lot of money."[30] A former high-ranking member of the NYPD said, "I don't think it works there. . . . They probably have a tiny file that nobody uses."[31]

The skepticism of these officers suggests the truth of their statements, for the opportunity to evade the registration requirements is always there. Informants can be rewarded without money provided by the department. Indeed, my own contacts with informants in New York suggested that the amounts that the department was willing to authorize were so pitifully small, no more than $25 for many purposes, that they made little difference to the informant. Officers could as easily fiddle with various expense accounts to cover disbursements of this size. Officers are surely right that informants are likely to be uneasy about being registered. If the officers are also reluctant, then we must assume that many evade the registration requirement. Given the secretive nature of police work involving informants, it is clearly difficult to prevent the recruitment of unreported informants.

If agents are to be prevented from licensing their informants, then it is necessary to formalize the relationship and the payments. The agent would have to record the informant's information so supervising officers could evaluate the consideration given the informant, in terms of either money or reduced charges. Such a procedure goes against very deeply ingrained customs of the police, who disdain paperwork (and who face more than enough of it when they have to process an arrest) and seek to control the information they collect in order to be able to gain the full reward from it. The tighter the requirement of formal control, the more likely the agent is to avoid registering informants.

The problem of formalizing agent-informant relations is embedded in the larger problems of information recording, informant "ownership," and information dissemination. Rubinstein (1973), dealing mostly with patrol and low-level vice officers, noted their reluctance to provide any information, even to their immediate supervisors, except when they were in a position to make use of it themselves. On the other hand, Williams et al. (1979) found that most narcotics units made serious efforts to prevent agents from acquiring restrictive control of an informant by requiring that other agents be introduced to the informant. My own contact with police intelligence activities suggests that the problem is a fundamental one. Police officers are rewarded for making cases, not for placing information in files where others can use it and take credit for it.

Limits of Reform

There is little we can do to change the current situation. Efforts to control informant-agent dealings will be counterproductive; they may force agents to conceal even more information and to find illegal ways of rewarding informants. Setting guidelines on the nature of licenses agents can issue to informants involves agencies in making policy statements about two very troubling activities. First, the agencies must clearly violate the law by stating that they will not arrest all criminals against whom they have information adequate to justify an arrest. Second, they must state a series of trade-offs which are certain to be contentious. Can a dealer who regularly makes one-ounce sales of heroin continue to operate if he provides good information against at least one four-ounce dealer every month? There is no correct answer to this question.

Moreover, any guidelines will open a new avenue of defense. Defendants may argue that they have been denied their opportunity to become licensed agents of the police. A one-ounce dealer may argue that prosecution is discriminatory, and may demand to see whether there is adequate representation of black or minority one-ounce dealers; are they given the same opportunities to work off charges as are white dealers? Due process requirements would surely be only a short step behind such guidelines. The judicial supervision of such requirements poses an enormous threat to the autonomy of police agencies in a very sensitive area of their work.

The enforceability of such guidelines, even outside of their due process implications, is also in question. The guidelines, in order to command public support, would probably specify fairly stringent requirements for informants. For agents, informants may be worth protecting even if they are less productive than the guidelines require. Given the ability of law enforcement agents to make informal deals, even across agencies, it may be difficult to ensure that only informants who meet the stringent requirements of the guidelines are in fact given license.

Are there no alternatives to unbridled discretion in the licensing of informants by police agencies and their individual agents? The problem is probably only potentially serious for federal agencies, simply because they have so much greater ability to protect their informants and are subject to so much greater pressure to make the kind of case that requires informants. The fragmentation of law enforcement in the United States over the last two decades has ensured that local police are neither motivated to issue broad licenses nor credible providers of them.

Moreover, the FBI and, to a lesser extent, the DEA, share characteristics that also suggest that the problem may not be too serious, i.e., that only occasionally are informants given very broad licenses, the nature of which would create public outcry if revealed. Unlike local police departments, the federal agencies are very much controlled by the flow of paper. FBI agents are required to account for their time in much more detail than their local counterparts.[32] Their supervisors are heavily involved in investigative decisions. The use of wiretaps in many major federal investigations also brings other agents into dealings with informants. None of these factors ensures that agent dealings with informants can be fully monitored, as Vilano's account suggests, but they do make it unlikely that many agents can enter into unmonitored arrangements with informants that involve the issuance of licenses much broader than the agency rules permit. In turn, agency executives are unlikely willingly to issue very broad licenses without promise of substantial returns, if only because of the risk that the agency runs from the runaway informant. Melvin Weinberg's behavior after the ABSCAM investigation provides a

114

salutary example.

Informants are perhaps the dirty secret of policing. Well-meaning efforts to impose tight controls on police dealings with informants are only likely to make for more secrecy and less effective control within the agencies. But policing is itself a dirty if necessary business, particularly in a nation which has chosen to prohibit the legal provision of so much that the public enjoys and to regulate the provision of so much else. If we wish to much reduce the police licensing of criminals, we must lower our expectations of what the police can do or change the legislation which permits criminals to profit so heavily from crimes without plaintiffs.

NOTES

1. The most notable early official statement of the significance of police discretion is The President's Commission on Law Enforcement and Administration of Justice, *The Challenge of Crime in a Free Society* (Washington, D.C.: U.S. Government Printing Office, 1967), p. 104.
2. The most precise statement is contained in chapter 3 of Kenneth Culp Davis, *Discretionary Justice* (Baton Rouge, La: University of Louisiana Press, 1969).
3. In chapter 4 of *Police Discretion* (St. Paul, Minn.: West Publishing, 1975), Kenneth Culp Davis argues that there is a legal foundation for such discretion if it is made openly. Though legislatures have passed full enforcement statutes, other, later, statutes clearly reflect an expectation of selective enforcement, as does the budgetary appropriation process.
4. An instance of this problem is provided in Herman Goldstein, *Policing in a Democratic Society* (Cambridge, Mass.: Ballinger, 1977).
5. The implications of this are discussed in James Q. Wilson, *The Varieties of Police Behavior* (Cambridge, Mass.: Harvard University Press, 1968).
6. A similar claim is made in Leroy Gould, et al., *Connections: Notes from the Heroin World* (New Haven: Yale University Press, 1974), p. 72.
7. Peter K. Manning, *The Narc's Game* (Cambridge, Mass.: MIT Press, 1980), p. 162.
8. "COINTELPRO, or the counterintelligence program, was a policy of disruption and harassment aimed at certain organizations deemed subversive, violent, or extremist. Usually, it involved FBI agents sending false and anonymous letters to organization members or to employers and newspapers designed to discredit a leader or his organization or to stimulate factional quarreling." James Q. Wilson, *The Investigators* (New York: Basic Books, 1978), p. 83.
9. *Ibid.,* p. 84.
10. Anthony Vilano, *Brick Agent* (New York: Ballantine Books, 1977), p. 96.
11. *Ibid.,* p. 116.
12. *Ibid.,* p. 112.
13. *Ibid.,* p. 116.
14. The wiretap application is listed as Document #79–0006/4–01/29–h of the United States District Court for the Western District of Missouri, Western Division. The case involved is discussed in U.S. Senate, *Organized Crime and the Use of Violence,* Hearings of the

Permanent Subcommittee of Investigation of the Senate Government Operations Committee, 96th Cong., 2d sess., April 30, 1980, p. 15.

15. I base this statement on conversations with a former federal prosecutor who said that the FBI was quite concerned when he referred to the Top Echelon program by name in the early 1970s. The program is mentioned in Sanford Ungar, *FBI: An Uncensored Look behind the Walls* (Boston: Little, Brown, 1975).

16. Ungar, *FBI,* p. 431, refers to the FBI's attitude that only its members can be trusted with confidential information. These beliefs were reflected in the passage of the Organized Crime Control Act of 1970, which took as its premise that illegal gambling flourished only because of the corruption of local police. Giving the FBI jurisdiction would at last lead to honest enforcement in gambling. See, "Remarks" of Senator Hruska, 115 *Congressional Record* 10736, 1969. The FBI has, however, been generally unwilling to investigate police corruption. See Herbert Beigel and Allan Beigel, *Beneath the Badge* (New York: Harper and Row, 1977).

17. Ungar, *FBI,* pp. 429–30, describes how the Bureau has used access to its training program to reward local officers it favors.

18. Manning, *The Narc's Game,* p. 247, presents figures on the amount spent on buys for various drugs. It appears that no more than three or four cases involved purchases of more than $1,000 worth of drugs. The average expenditure per arrest was only $61.45.

19. Robert Daley, *Prince of the City* (Boston: Houghton Mifflin, 1978), p. 243.

20. Wilson, *The Investigators,* pp. 21–23.

21. Epstein (1977, p. 106) does report a Baltimore narcotics officer's claiming 800 dealer informants with de facto franchises, presumably most issued by local police.

22. Jay Williams, et al., *Police Narcotics Control: Patterns and Strategies* (Washington, D.C.: National Institute of Justice, 1979), chapter 5.

23. Department of Justice, "Attorney General's Guidelines on FBI Use of Informants and Confidential Sources" (Mimeo), December 2, 1980.

24. *Ibid.,* p. 8

25. *Ibid.,* p. 9.

26. General Accounting Office, "FBI Audit Conclusions on the Criminal Informant Program Should Have Been Qualified," Report GGD–80–37 (Washington, D.C.: March 13, 1980).

27. "FBI officials do not believe a confidential questionnaire would have provided more reliable data. They note that few agents would respond differently to such a questionnaire because they would not believe their responses would be kept confidential." *Ibid.,* p. 6.

28. *Ibid.,* p. 4.

29. *Ibid.,* p. 23.

30. David Kleinman, "Out of the Shadows and Into the Files: Who Should Control Informants?" *Police Magazine,* November 1980, p. 40.

31. *Ibid.,* p. 9.

32. See Wilson, *The Investigators,* pp. 91–108.

REFERENCES

Beigel, Herbert and Allan Beigel. *Beneath the Badge.* New York: Harper and Row, 1977.

Daley, Robert. *Prince of the City.* Boston, Mass.: Houghton Mifflin, 1978.

Davis, Kenneth Culp. *Discretionary Justice.* Baton Rouge, La.: University of Louisiana Press, 1969.

116

————. *Police Discretion.* St. Paul, Minn.: West Publishing, 1975.

Epstein, Edward Jay. *Agency of Fear.* New York: G.P. Putnam, 1977.

General Accounting Office. "FBI Audit Conclusions on the Criminal Informant Program Should Have Been Qualified." Report GGD–80–37, Washington, D.C., March 13, 1980.

Goldstein, Herman. *Policing in a Democratic Society.* Cambridge, Mass.: Ballinger, 1977.

Goldstein, Joseph. "Police Discretion Not to Invoke the Criminal Process: Low-Visibility Decisions in the Administration of Justice." 69 *Yale Law Journal:* 543–96 (March 1960).

Gould, Leroy, Andrew Walker, Lansing Crane, and Charles Lidz. *Connections: Notes from the Heroin World.* New Haven, Conn.: Yale University Press, 1974.

Greenwood, Peter et al. *The Criminal Investigation Process.* Santa Monica, Calif.: The Rand Corporation, 1975.

Kleinman, David. "Out of the Shadows and Into the Files: Who Should Control Informants?" *Police Magazine,* November 1980.

Manning, Peter K. *The Narc's Game.* Cambridge, Mass.: MIT Press, 1980.

President's Commission on Law Enforcement and Administration of Justice. *The Challenge of Crime in a Free Society.* Washington, D.C.: U.S. Government Printing Office, 1967.

Reuter, Peter. *Markets and the Mafia: The Economics of the Visible Hand.* Cambridge, Mass.: MIT Press, 1983.

Skolnick, Jerome. *Justice Without Trial.* New York: John Wiley and Sons, 1966.

Ungar, Sanford. *The FBI: An Uncensored Look Behind the Walls.* Boston, Mass.: Little, Brown, 1975.

Vilano, Anthony. *Brick Agent.* New York: Ballantine Books, 1977.

Williams, Jay et al. *Police Narcotics Control: Patterns and Strategies.* Washington, D.C.: National Institute of Justice, 1979.

Wilson, James Q. *The Varieties of Police Behavior.* Cambridge, Mass.: Harvard University Press, 1968.

————. *The Investigators.* New York: Basic Books, 1978.

6

From Whodunit to Who Does It:
Fairness and Target Selection
In Deceptive Investigations

Lawrence W. Sherman*

THE POLITICAL DEBATE OVER THE FBI's ABSCAM investigation of the U.S. Congress has raised a number of important moral questions. Should lies and deception be used at all in criminal investigations? If they are, what safeguards should be employed to protect those who pass the test of honesty by refusing to engage in crime? And since exposure to

---

* Paper presented to the Conference of Police Ethics, John Jay College of Criminal Justice, City University of New York, April 24, 1982.

contrived opportunities to commit crime is (at the least) a major intrusion into someone's life, how should targets for such investigations be selected?

These questions have been around for centuries, but no one has paid them much heed. Police have been using deception to investigate prostitutes, gamblers, bootleggers, homosexuals, and dope pushers, but few observers have ever shown much moral outrage about applying the techniques to targets of such low social status. Once the same methods were applied to high public officials, however, the moral questions received a great deal of attention.[1]

This chapter addresses the question of how targets for deceptive investigations should be selected. It sets aside the question of whether such investigations should be conducted at all, in part because that question seems moot, given the widespread police use of deception. It does address the issue of safeguarding the innocent because that is one of the benefits of adopting a more systematic approach to target selection.

The Equity of Deceptive Investigations

Most of our notions of fair play in the Anglo-American tradition of law enforcement assume a reactive system, with a fairly rigid time-ordering of events. First an offense is committed. Then the offense or evidence of the offense is observed by a victim or bystander. The victim or observer openly accuses the suspect, and the accusation is contested in the open adversarial process of a courtroom trial. The system of law enforcement is reactive in this model because it does nothing but react to an accusation that a crime has already occurred. In determining "whodunit," the system emphasizes the past tense of the verb. All our notions of due process, discovery of evidence, right to confront accusers, refusal to admit hearsay, and others stem from this conception of law enforcement focused on events that have occurred in the past.

But in a complex society, the more important crimes may be those that continue to occur. Law enforcement faces great challenges in the present tense, as well as in the past tense: catching who *does* it, not just who has *done* it. This is not a significant distinction for crimes that occur in public. The crazed sniper who shoots at passers-by for several hours is a present-tense criminal the police have no trouble locating, apprehend-

119

ing, or gathering evidence on. But crimes that occur in private may continue for years without anyone ever knowing about them, or without any direct evidence ever surfacing.

A strictly reactive system of law enforcement is, therefore, an inherently unfair system. While it may be the foundation of our hallowed traditions of civil liberties, it creates for the rich and poor unequal chances of being caught. Those people who commit crimes in public, or who by the very nature of their crimes are more likely to leave observable evidence, are the most likely to be caught and punished. Those people who have the power and wealth to commit crimes in private, in ways that do not create a self-defined "victim," are the least likely to be punished (Reiss and Bordua, 1967). A reactive system is hopelessly biased against those who are unprotected by the institutions of privacy, a social good which is unequally distributed according to wealth and power (Stinchcombe, 1963).

The alternative is a system blind to the distinctions among crimes and people created by social inequalities. A proactive system of law enforcement (Reiss, 1971) does not depend upon complaints from self-defined victims in order to launch an investigation. Rather, based on a general belief that a certain kind of crime is occurring in a certain place, among a certain group of people, or at the hand of one particular individual, police can employ a variety of tactics to gather the evidence necessary for arrest and prosecution. These tactics need not be deceptive. Mere surveillance from a public place, or the examination of financial records, or the persuasion of a participant to confess are possible tactics of proactive investigations (Sherman, 1978). But very often the most effective tactics are based on deception: a police agent claiming to be a narcotics dealer, or a prospective customer for a prostitute's services, or an Arab businessman attempting to obtain special immigration status.

Is deception necessary? Many would argue the point. Critics of wiretaps, for example, have claimed that they are a symptom of police laziness; the police could solve many more crimes by doing the good solid police work of interviews of witnesses and gathering physical evidence. This view may be unrealistic. While there is scant empirical evidence on the question, I know of no major successful prosecution of corruption or other important secretive, "victimless crimes" in which the

120

evidence was not gathered through a deceptive use of undercover agents, informers, a traitor among the participants in the crime, or some other way of persuading the criminal to commit the crime in the presence of others in the mistaken belief that it was safe to do so.

It appears that deception is the only way to even up the score between the rich and the poor criminals, the public and the private, the past-tense and the present-tense criminals. The price of the equity deception makes possible is the loss of privacy, as well as the loss of trust deception engenders. There is a tragic choice to be made between equity of punishment for crime and the rights to privacy and non-deception. For centuries that choice has been made in favor of privacy, which is a de facto choice in favor of the middle and upper classes; the lower classes were exposed to deception in public. Even those who cherish privacy and non-deception most dearly may want to consider whether this is the proper choice for public policy.

The ABSCAM investigation and the work of former New York City corruption prosecutor, Maurice Nadjari, may be viewed as public policy experiments in the opposite choice. They exposed high public officials to deceptive invasions of privacy, providing an opportunity to commit a crime under observation. They have been criticized for sacrificing the value of privacy, but rarely praised for contributing to greater equity. This reaction is probably correct. For until the methods of selecting priorities and individual targets of proactive, deceptive investigations become much more open and demonstrably fair, they will remain vulnerable to charges of being "witch hunts," "fishing expeditions," or "personal vendettas."

Proactive investigations only have the potential to increase the equity of law enforcement. They have not yet achieved that potential.

Probable Cause and Sampling Theory

The greatest obstacle to achieving equitable law enforcement through deceptive investigations is an overly restrictive conception of "probable cause." This term is used at law most often as the evidentiary standard needed for making an arrest. The evidentiary standard needed for starting an investigation has been labeled a "reasonable, articulable suspicion." But in his comments on the ABSCAM investigation, FBI

Director William Webster said, "We're only investigating people who we have *reason to believe* are engaged or would like to engage in a crime." (Washington *Post,* March 22, 1982, p. A2). And in his comments on having been selected as a target of the ABSCAM investigation, Rep. William J. Hughes of New Jersey (about whom no evidence of wrongdoing was apparently found) said that if the FBI fails to provide him with sufficient information to indicate why he was a target, he may file a lawsuit.

These comments address the crucial question about deceptive investigations: On what criteria should investigative targets be selected? The legalistic answer these comments suggest is this: Targets should be selected on the basis of specific facts already in hand about specific people.

This answer defeats the major purpose of deceptive investigations. It is tantamount to saying, "Unless you have evidence, you may not obtain evidence," a Catch-22 that could have major consequences. The worst consequence is that it limits the potential for making law enforcement more equitable across different types of crimes and different classes of people. This argument is clearly supported by an examination of the process by which tips, clues, or other preliminary evidence come to the attention of police, in light of what statisticians call sampling theory.

The reactive model of law enforcement assumes that evidence about crimes becomes available by a random process. People committing crimes make mistakes, or good citizens shoulder their public responsibility to report offenses. Some discussions even imply that all crimes produce evidence.[2]

In sampling theory, this premise would be described as evidence providing an unbiased sample of all crimes. Even if evidence does not surface on all crimes, the tips or leads that do emerge should be fairly representative of the entire "universe" of crimes. Since law enforcement resources are limited anyway, the argument is that they should be allocated according to tips received.

This model makes about as much sense as relying on mail sent to the White House as a sample of public opinion about the president. Public opinion analysts know that people who write letters are different from other people. What they write is not a representative sample of public opinion, but rather a biased sample: a sample correlated with all

122

those factors that make some people write letters while most people don't. In the same way, crimes about which some evidence surfaces are different from crimes for which evidence does not surface.

Leon Mayhew (1968) demonstrated this point in his study of the Massachusetts Commission Against Discrimination (MCAD). He discovered a paradox in the MCAD's pattern of enforcement: the companies with the best institutional records of hiring on an equal opportunity basis were subjected to the greatest number of MCAD investigations. Those companies with the worst records were relatively untouched. Why? Because the companies that hired minorities then became vulnerable to charges of discrimination in promotion, and even in hiring as the word spread that minorities could get jobs at those firms. The companies that kept minorities out had few minorities even apply, and still fewer to complain about discrimination in promotions.

Because the MCAD was guided by the complaints it received, it went after the wrong targets. Instead of fighting discrimination where it was most widespread, the MCAD punished the firms whose offenses were the least serious. That kind of mistaken target selection is the result of assuming that the tips or evidence presented to an investigative agency constitute an unbiased sample of the criminal population.

A much more equitable enforcement strategy would have been for the MCAD to select a random sample of all companies of a certain size. These companies could then be "tested" deceptively (just as real estate agents are tested by civil rights groups in many cities) to see whether whites and blacks of equal qualifications receive the same treatment and job offers. Or even without deception, the investigators could examine in detail the sampled companies' records and statistics on the number of applicants, employees, and promotions by race or other protected category. The method of investigation is not crucial; the method of selecting the target is.

The random sample of a predefined list (or "universe") of all companies of a certain size has a much greater likelihood of providing an unbiased sample of discrimination in employment than a sample that is based solely on public complaints. Any sample drawn at random—or according to a mathematically derived table of random numbers, a very systematic procedure not to be confused with a haphazard method like

123

pulling names out of a hat—is more likely to be representative of a larger universe than a sample drawn by any other method. So if the goal of an MCAD is to attack and penalize discrimination in jobs, the most effective method for finding discrimination to attack is not to sit back and wait for a tip. The most effective method is to go out and look for the problem, using the random sampling selection procedure.

The same would be true for almost any kind of crime. Indeed, the very counting of crimes in our society has moved from total reliance on victim complaints (as recorded in the FBI's Uniform Crime Reports) to the addition of randomly sampled interviews of the entire population asking whether people have been victimized by crime (in the Census Bureau's National Crime Survey). Not surprisingly, the two methods of counting crime have produced very different pictures of the trends and distribution of crime. It would seem to be a small step from random samples for counting crime to random samples for choosing targets for investigating crime. But a thousand years of Anglo-American tradition binds us to a conception of justice as redress for individual victims, a mechanism for personal revenge rather than a tool of social regulation through deterrence. When the federal Equal Employment Opportunity Commission during the Carter administration attempted to divert resources from investigating complaints to broader investigations of job discrimination patterns, it was attacked by civil rights groups, and the plan was thwarted. Our allegiance to the "justice as vengeance" notion is strong.

In the area of white-collar crime and corruption, the justice as vengeance model is even stronger. While we have little empirical data, my impression is that secretive, ongoing criminal conspiracies get revealed only when conflicts develop among the participants. This pattern appears often in the area of police corruption (Sherman, 1978) and may apply more broadly. "Dropping a dime" has always been an excellent way to get revenge on people, especially when they are innocent. Newark Police Director Hubert Williams suffered through several investigations by the state attorney general's office because the police union, with whom Williams was at odds over policy matters, tried to punish him by sending in false tips and accusations to the attorney general. The attorney general's office has a policy of investigating every complaint, so the

124

vengeance was quite effective, at least as harassment.

Two conclusions emerge from examining current criteria for mobilizing investigations. One is that relying on tips and other citizen-initiated methods of obtaining probable cause to start an investigation is a wasteful and inequitable procedure. It results in selecting targets who might be the last ones selected if investigators could know the full scope of criminal activity. Worst of all, it allows investigators to become the tool of personal vengeance rather than an instrument of public policy.

The second conclusion is that some sort of representative sample of an entire population (or universe of potential criminals) is a preferable procedure for selecting targets for investigations aimed at non-public crimes. This conclusion raises two problems. The first is whether it is right and proper to initiate an investigation without any specific information about specific individuals. The second problem is how the random sampling procedure could actually be used in practice in a fair manner to increase the equitability of law enforcement.

Group Probabilities and Individual Targets

Consider the morality of investigating people without specific evidence that they are committing crimes.

There are two ways to generate hunches about who might be committing crimes in secret. One is to obtain information about specific individuals. The other is to obtain information—or even inferences— that a certain group of people is, or is likely to be, committing certain kinds of crime. By deduction, any individual who belongs to a group is as likely (absent additional information) as any other individual to be guilty of the crime. Information or inferences about the existence of criminal activities in groups can therefore provide a starting point for investigating individual group members. But is it right to proceed in that fashion?

Consider the question not in the abstract, but in concrete examples of current practices. Few people complain when they are stopped by a roadblock after a convicted murderer escapes from prison. Yet they are being subjected to an investigation solely on the basis of their group membership: they belong to the group of people driving cars within a certain radius of the prison, any one of whom could be, by logical inference, the escaped killer.

Few people complain when they are forced by customs agents to open their suitcases for inspection on returning from a trip abroad. Yet they (and not their neighbors back home) are being subjected to investigation only because they belong to the group of people who are in the most logical position to be smuggling drugs or other contraband: people who are traveling from abroad.

Some people have objected to, but still cooperate with, the recent practice of some police departments enforcing the laws against drunk driving. Roadblocks are established so that every driver who passes the checkpoint is stopped and given a breathalyzer test. If the driver fails the test, then he or she may be arrested for drunken driving. Yet there is no more probable cause for initiating that investigation than the fact that many drivers are drunk, as the post-mortems from fatal accidents prove. The investigation of the drivers who encounter those roadblocks is premised solely on the fact that they belong to the group of people who drive.

Apply the same principle to employment discrimination. If many companies have hundreds of employees, all of whom are white males, then it is a likely (if not conclusive) inference that some companies engage in systematic discrimination. Indeed, that is why the MCAD was established in the first place. If the roadblock/border principle is correct, then the MCAD should have sufficient probable cause to investigate all companies or any company selected in a truly random fashion. (This is virtually the same thing. Both an every-member-of-the population sample and a random sample of one-tenth of the population gives each member of the population an equal chance of being selected.)

Apply the principle to Congress or the judiciary. If some members of Congress or judges have been found guilty of corruption in the past, that is reasonable evidence for inferring that some members of those population groups may be committing the same crimes now. The roadblock/border principle suggests that this is sufficient probable cause for launching an investigation against all, or a random sample of, members of Congress or judges.

We recoil from the idea of investigating people for no reason, a practice which smacks of a police state. We also recoil from the idea of investigating individuals on the whim of an official, with all the personal

126

prejudices and desires for vengeance that might shape that decision. That smacks of abuse of public power for personal goals. These are the two main reasons we have required articulable suspicions about specific people as a prerequisite for initiating some, but not all (such as roadblocks) investigations. But these are negative reasons, not a positive ethical principle, for guiding the selection of investigative targets.

The principle I suggest is that police should investigate someone only when that person has a higher probability than the general population of committing a crime. This principle is both ethically defensible and practical. People with the same probability as everyone else, or lower, should not be harassed by police, nor would it be productive to investigate them. The whole point of tips or complaints is to induce the conclusion of a higher probability for one person and not to provide final proof sufficient for a conviction. If the same increase in probability could be deduced with equal or greater accuracy, then it should be an equally valid procedure. Given good information about which groups of people are likely to be committing crimes, I would even predict that deductive target selection through random sampling is more productive than inductive target selection through tips and complaints.

What is needed to make inductive target selection acceptable is a procedure that protects against investigating individuals for no reason at all (a true fishing expedition) or investigating people because of the personal biases of the police. As Donald Black (1973) has observed, a reactive law enforcement system is heavily biased, but the biases are democratic: they are open to influence by all the people. A proactive law enforcement system, by contrast, has the potential to be unbiased, but the outcome is no longer in the hands of the people. Since we are probably unwilling to entrust such grave powers solely to police officials, we should consider a system that is both equitable and democratically accountable. The procedure must be accountable at two separate stages: the selection of groups for investigation, and the selection of individual targets within those groups.

Group Priorities For Deceptive Investigations

My proposal for using deceptive investigations to make law enforcement more equitable begins with a three-point plan for selecting target

127

groups. The groups should be selected through a process of administrative rulemaking, and priorities should be set in the same way. The criteria for selecting the groups should be spelled out and debated in this process, along with the actual selection. Finally, all target groups should be given fair notice and warning that they could be exposed to deceptive investigations once a decision has been reached.

Administrative Rulemaking

Every law enforcement agency has its hunches about where and among which groups secretive crimes are being committed. If the agency wants to use deceptive methods to investigate people in those groups, it could be held accountable for that decision by announcing its intention to do so and seeking public comment. If it were a federal law enforcement agency, the plan could be published in the *Federal Register*. Local agencies could take a legal advertisement in the newspaper and hold hearings.

The advantage of this procedure is that it gets the public involved in what is inherently a process of making tragic choices among competing values. No police agency has sufficient resources to investigate all offenses or all groups suspected of committing the offenses. They all must set priorities. In doing so, they may attempt to mirror the values of their communities at large. In either case, it is appropriate for any interested persons to be allowed to comment.

There are at least two disadvantages to the administrative rulemaking procedure. One is that it forces the agency to sacrifice the advantage of surprise. This is an unavoidable cost of giving fair notice and public involvement; the one value precludes the other. The way to minimize the problem is to frame the target groups in sufficiently general categories that no one can be certain exactly where the deceptive investigations will be undertaken. Categories as general as "public officials" would be preferable to categories as specific as "building inspectors."

A second disadvantage is that the responses to the proposed set of priorities will constitute a biased sample of public opinion just as surely as a set of public complaints would. Only this set of biases would be different. It would be biased in favor of people who enjoy the visibility and the process of trying to influence public policy, such as professors and lawyers. It would also be biased in favor of those whose ox is to be gored.

128

If public officials are the target, then no doubt the public officials' unions will lobby intensively to reverse that decision. If grain shipping companies or trucking companies are the target, then the trade associations for those industries would rally round the process to reverse the decision.

Such lobbying efforts can be formidable. The experience of federal regulatory agencies with administrative rulemaking might support the view that they are captives of the industries they are intended to regulate. But not all regulatory agencies are alike in this respect. Some are much more prone to take a public interest viewpoint (if Congress lets them) than the viewpoint of those who lobby for their own interests.

With proper safeguards, it might be possible to construct an administrative rulemaking procedure for police agencies that afforded independence from the lobbying of the target groups. That is not to say the target groups should be ignored in such a process. Rather, their arguments should be considered on their merits rather than because of the political influence they carry behind them.

Criteria for Priority-Setting

The administrative rulemaking process will be less vulnerable to improper influences if the criteria for selecting crimes and population groups are made explicit. These criteria need not be quantifiable. But if they can be clearly articulated, they can provide a standard against which both agency-suggested priorities and public comment on them can be evaluated.

One standard might be the *number of lives lost* in a criminal activity. By this standard, drunken driving might become the highest priority for deceptive investigations. Drunk drivers kill three times as many people as "intentional" murderers. Police could place undercover agents in bars and observe people drinking, arresting and breathalyzing them if they start to drive too soon after drinking.

A more subtle lives-lost criterion might be the rate of death caused per action. By this standard, drug dealers would probably be a higher priority for deceptive investigations than drunk drivers; the number of murders per narcotics transaction is probably higher than the number of deaths caused by each incident of drunk driving. Deceptive investigations of narcotics dealing are already well established, but that is no reason not to articulate the criteria for conducting them and giving them a higher priority than some other types of investigations.

Another criterion for setting priorities might be the *amount of money stolen* or property lost in an activity. Here again, one faces a choice between aggregate losses and the loss rate per incident. Shoplifting and employee theft, for example, produce large aggregate losses, but the amount of loss per theft incident is usually quite small. Large corporate "Ponzi" schemes rarely happen, but the losses they cause through fraud are enormous.

A third criterion for setting priorities would be the *degree of threat to democratic government* the criminal activity poses. A city council member taking bribes to alter votes on zoning ordinances may pose a greater threat than a police officer taking bribes from prostitutes, although these distinctions must be heavily value-laden. Indeed, many people objected to the ABSCAM investigations precisely because the sale of immigration privileges poses such a limited threat to the democratic process. Had the subject of the investigation been something like accepting bribes to influence foreign policy or budgetary decisions, ABSCAM would have been more justified under this criterion.

These are only three possible criteria, although others may be useful. The major problem for the rulemaking process will be how to combine or rank-order the competing criteria for setting priorities. To my mind, the lives-lost and threat-to-government criteria are equal contenders for first place, with property loss a clear second. But each law enforcement agency may represent communities with different values (Goldstein, 1977), and each should be allowed to determine its own rank-order criteria.

Due Notice

Whatever the selection criteria, the target groups selected should be given proper notice that they may be exposed to deceptive investigations affording them the opportunity to commit crimes under law enforcement observation. If the target population is drunk drivers, then the law enforcement agency should take out a large advertisement in the newspaper. If the target population is public officials in a city government, then letters of notice should be sent to all public officials.

There are several reasons for providing due notice. One is that it makes the process of deception fairer. Publishing the rules of the game in advance is fairer play than changing the rules in the middle of the game. Equally important, perhaps, is the deterrent effect of the due notice procedure. The notice may deter more criminal activity (at least in some population groups) than the investigations and sanctions. If there were never any investigations to back up the notices, however, the deterrent effect of the notices might wither away.

The most important ethical reason for providing due notice is to remove any stigma from those people who are tested and commit no crime. Current investigations leave such people implicated by vague press publicity about having been a target in the investigation. That phrase implies that they must have been doing something wrong, or else they would not have been a target. Some people involved in the ABSCAM investigation, for example, suffered severe consequences; one was divorced by his wife, two attempted suicide, and one lost all of his business clients in reaction to the stigma.

Due notice to a group in itself might not remove the stigma from those who are selected as targets. As long as people presume that tips or other evidence of probable cause about specific individuals are prerequisites for investigation, then "target" status will necessarily carry some stigma. But if everyone knew that targets were randomly selected, and that becoming an investigative target was no more disreputable than being audited by the IRS (even less so), then the unfair attachment of stigma to the innocent could be avoided.

Individual Target Selection

Once a target population group with a higher-than-average probability of committing a particular crime has been selected, the next administrative problem must be dealt with. That problem is selecting individual targets for deceptive investigations in a way that gives each member of the target group an equal probability of being selected. As argued earlier, this procedure is preferable to relying on tips or even the reputation of certain individuals. But for some kinds of crimes, it will be difficult to identify the universe of individuals who belong to that higher-than-average probability group.

131

There are many well-defined groups from which an individual sample can be drawn. Members of Congress, the judiciary, or municipal agencies can all be selected on the basis of a random numbers formula to be investigative targets. A list of their names is readily accessible so that they can be numbered and selected according to the formula. This almost guarantees each member of the population will have an equal chance of being selected.

But for other kinds of crime, the procedure cannot be nearly as orderly. There is no official list of people who are potential drug dealers. Nor is there a list of people selling other kinds of contraband in private. For this kind of crime, enforcement may have no other option than to rely on tips.

But there are many higher than average probability population groups that fall between the total secrecy of contraband sales and the total visibility of official employment. Business corporations and the names of their officers are registered with state governments. Prostitutes, drunk drivers, and people carrying weapons illegally are all part of the population group on the streets and could be sampled visually and selected on a random basis, rather than on a police officer's instincts about who looks suspicious.[3]

The details of the sampling procedure would vary for each group, but the principle of equal probability of selection is widely applicable. Corporations could be randomly selected for deceptive investigations of compliance with tax or antitrust laws. Real estate companies could be randomly selected for deceptive investigations of compliance with antidiscrimination laws.

Conclusion

That is not to say that deception ought to be used to investigate all these crimes. Deception is a powerful and intrusive tool; its use still strikes many as repugnant. It is the failure to use it, however, that produces the inequities in our system of justice. It is the failure to use deception that distorts the statistics on race and crime, making poor blacks appear more prone to crime than rich whites. It is the failure to equalize law enforcement through deception that puts poor blacks in prison for stealing $70 while whites commit tax evasion and other financial frauds without ever risking an investigation, much less a prison term.

Moreover, if these crimes are going to be investigated at all—especially with deception—then the only fair way to select targets is by random sampling. The current method of relying on tips and leads unfairly implicates the innocent and may miss some of the most serious criminals. Target selection by deduction from group membership is far more in keeping with the spirit of equal protection of the law and equal risk of punishment than induction from rumor and hearsay.

ABSCAM was the starting case in point for this discussion. What may apply to investigations of the Congress or other public officials may not apply to crimes committed by others. The very notion of a "population group of above-average probability of committing a particular crime" may smack of racism or other prejudices. But the fact remains that only members of Congress can sell congressional votes, and only judges can sell judicial decisions. It is in that sense that they belong to population groups with above-average probabilities of committing offenses. And if some of their number are to be investigated, then it would be fairer to all concerned to replace current methods of target selection with the random selection process proposed here.

NOTES

1. Perhaps journalists, public policy analysts, and philosophers, like police, also need to consider moral standards for selecting the targets of their inquiry to avoid such inequitable concern for the welfare of the powerful.

2. An alternative implication is that if it does not produce evidence, it should not be investigated. This is a defensible position in terms of the value of privacy, but not in terms of the value of equity.

3. After enough random selection has been accomplished, it could be possible to construct a systematic profile of the characteristics most often associated with the people found to be committing the crime. This empirically derived profile would be less biased than an officer's hunch.

REFERENCES

Black, Donald. "The Mobilization of Law." *Journal of Legal Studies* 2:125–49, 1973.

Goldstein, Herman. *Policing A Free Society.* Cambridge, Mass.: Ballinger, 1977.

Mayhew, Leon. *Law and Equal Opportunity.* Cambridge, Mass.: Harvard University Press, 1973.

Reiss, Albert J., Jr. *The Police and the Public.* New Haven, Conn.: Yale University Press, 1971.

————and David J. Bordua. "Environment and Organization: A Perspective on the Police." in *The Police: Six Sociological Essays,* ed. David J. Bordua. New York: John Wiley, 1967, pp. 25–55.

Sherman, Lawrence W. *Scandal and Reform: Controlling Police Corruption.* Berkeley and Los Angeles: University of California Press, 1978.

Stinchcombe, Arthur L. "Institutions of Privacy in the Determination of Police Administrative Practice," *American Journal of Sociology* 69:150–60, 1963.

7

Undercover Investigations:
An Administrative Perspective

Wayne A. Kerstetter

PUBLIC AND PROFESSIONAL CRITICISM OF both the priorities and the effectiveness of police, restrictions on use of search warrants, and increased difficulty in obtaining convictions without direct testimony have led, in the past decade, to a tendency among police agencies toward "proactive" policing technologies.[1] One of these techniques is the increased use of undercover investigators for a variety of criminal activities.

Many of the crimes that are the focus of these investigations are complainantless in the sense that no one comes forward to report a crime and to bear witness to it. Such crimes include, for example, transactions between retailers and wholesalers of drugs or counterfeit money or between burglars and dealers in stolen property, or the bribery of a public official by a person willing to pay for the favorable exercise of official discretion. Because these crimes are lucrative and attract middle- and upper-class individuals, police attention to them was often urged as a matter of social equity.[2] But because these crimes involve two willing parties, a major source of evidence—"knowledgeable witnesses"— normally is denied to the police. As a result, the police developed tactics which involve entering into the criminal transaction by a police-directed informant or undercover police officer. These tactics have led to the criticism that the police are practicing deception and that they are "creating" crime.[3] This chapter suggests a particular analytic approach to the issues involved in using these techniques, an approach that differs from much of the public and legal discussion of such issues. The analysis includes an examination of the major investigative alternatives in complainantless crimes, and concludes with some observations about the nature of the value choices involved.

An Administrative Perspective

From an administrative perspective, much of the public discussion about law enforcement strategies and tactics is unproductive, usually because the discussion takes place out of context. These controversies almost inevitably concern the balancing of competing social values that are, and properly should be, political issues in a most fundamental sense. They represent the need to make appropriate allocations of power between the state and the individual.[4] The appropriateness of any particular allocation depends ultimately on the values of the society making the allocation.

Thus law enforcement administrators must consider such issues in the context not only of the social institutions, interests, and values which the tactics are intended to protect, but also within a realistic consideration of the likely effectiveness and potential costs of alternative tactics.[5]

Characteristics of Complainantless Crimes

While inquiry into the social desirability of a particular law enforcement technique should begin with as precise a definition as possible of the nature and severity of the threat it is to combat, this effort is often impeded by lack of specific and verifiable information.

When a victim or other citizen reports a crime, the police can then analyze the information and come up with an investigative blueprint for that specific crime. When we are dealing with complainantless crime, however, no such clear path emerges. The police are often generally aware of a problem but do not have specific information on which to act. Although there may be victims, often they are confused about what has happened, and even unsure about whether a crime actually has occurred. In trying to investigate this type of crime, police usually have little to go on but rumor, innuendo, and suspicious circumstances. Even the likely sources of information are suspect because of their own involvement in criminal activity.

This is particularly true in the case of public officials. Allegations of misconduct against public officials that are specific enough to merit investigation tend to come from informants who themselves are involved in the alleged misconduct or have engaged in other criminal activities. The information they provide may be detailed but it is usually hard to verify because it involves conversations or cash payments of which no record exists. Law enforcement officials who undertake to pursue such information face the prospect, at trial, of a swearing contest between an informant who admits involvement in criminal activity and a respected public official. Without substantial corroboration, the testimony of the informant would be useless. But where to find the corroboration?

Initiating an investigation into accusations against a member of a different branch of government or of a different political allegiance exposes the law enforcement administrator to charges of engaging in politically motivated harassment as well as to retaliation from power centers allied with the official under investigation. Further, concerns about separation of powers and an awareness that all public officials are subject to unscrupulous attacks by people with a variety of motivations cause the conscientious law enforcement administrator to proceed cautiously. Despite these difficulties, the allegations at times explain the patterns of behavior of the accused official. In these circumstances, the law enforcement official faces a difficult choice as to how to respond to the allegations, especially when the allegations concern serious misconduct by senior officials.

The dilemma is exacerbated by the perception that the problem is pervasive. The former U.S. Attorney for the Northern District of Illinois, Thomas Sullivan, much of whose career has been as a defense attorney, may well have been reflecting such concerns when, in his public statement summarizing his experience upon leaving office, he said:

> In one sense, my experience as United States Attorney has been disheartening. There seems to be in Chicago and the surrounding areas a pervasive, deep-seated lack of honesty at all levels of government and business. I do not know whether it is worse here than elsewhere, but I do know that public and private corruption is commonplace in our city.
>
> The justification cannot be found in community acceptance or tacit approval. The corruption operates in stealth and secrecy, and when it is exposed in court the juries almost always convict. Those jurors share the sense of outrage and frustration we feel when we uncover these misdeeds. And we know in our bones that the cases which reach the courts represent only a tiny fraction of the whole.[6]

Mr. Sullivan's view accurately reflects the perceptions of many law enforcement officials. His recommendation was that "each of us must renew personal dedication to integrity and be willing to tell the authorities to get involved when we encounter fraud and corruption, whether it be public or private. Clearly that is the best answer. Yet, considering the costs in time and effort, the possibilities for direct or indirect retaliation by those involved or their friends, and widespread distaste (even contempt) for the "squealer," can society rely upon individual citizens' action on the basis of personal integrity as its main line of defense? The short- and long-term costs to the person who comes forward to bear witness are substantial, and there is relatively little the authorities can do to ease these burdens, particularly over the long term.

The concept of jurisdiction is also problematic in complainantless crime. The retail trade, whether of counterfeit money or illegal drugs, may be local, but higher level transactions take place across city, state, and national boundaries. Large-scale theft operations also tend to retail their wares far from the location of the original crime. Thus the notion of

138

location, for purposes of police planning and allocation of resources, is very different for these types of crime than for muggings, for example.

Further, the usefulness of physical evidence in establishing the occurrence and location of a criminal incident varies with crime type. For drugs and counterfeit money the production and possession of contraband are temporal events of substantial duration that allow police to seize them as physical evidence. Physical evidence of bribery is more difficult to obtain. The money that is exchanged, unless carefully marked or recorded (serial numbers), is of little value and need not remain long in the immediate possession of the individuals involved.

These characteristics of complainantless crimes make traditional police techniques such as preventive patrol, interviews of victims and witnesses, and record searches either inefficient or ineffective, or both. They make it difficult to know if, when, and where to initiate an investigation and how to pursue it once initiated.

Although determining the extent of complainantless crime is difficult, the importance of threats to social values and institutions is clear. The danger to the integrity of a national currency from unrestrained counterfeiting is undeniable. The social consequences to a democratic nation of the unbridled corruption of public officials are manifest.

Investigative Options

The enforcement of laws against counterfeiting provides an interesting example of investigative options because the presence of physical evidence for a substantial period of time and the existence of a complainant at some point in the series of transactions allows for use of a wider range of investigative techniques than in other crimes, such as corruption.

Techniques generally available to police for obtaining evidence of complainantless crimes are:

- apprehension in the act
- visual surveillance
- electronic surveillance
- search warrants

- informant testimony
- co-conspirator testimony
- undercover agent testimony

In the case of counterfeiting, apprehension of the offender in the act is possible but infrequent. It requires both substantial alertness on the part of the intended victim and some resources for holding the offender until the authorities arrive. Offenders thus apprehended usually are low-level operatives or retailers. To expand the investigation to wholesalers and producers generally requires the cooperation of the retailers, and it is seldom forthcoming without some rewards, usually in the form of prosecutorial or judicial leniency. The promise of leniency or even immunity implies an offer to restrain or ameliorate the impact of the criminal law on the offender. One does not have to subscribe to the analysis proffered by Misner and Clough[7] (that use of possible legal sanctions to induce an arrestee to work as an informant is a form of peonage proscribed by the Thirteenth Amendment) to be troubled by the ethical problems of that practice. There is a very real threat of physical harm to the person who serves as an informant, as well as the potential for psychological damage as a consequence of the role played. The difficulty of that role is reflected in the pejorative language the police themselves use in describing informants.

Failing catching the offender in the act, the police might use visual surveillance in their efforts to enforce the counterfeiting laws. The first question is whom should the police watch?[8] A description of the offender from a victim may be helpful, but a victim (say a bank teller) may not know which of many customers passed the counterfeit bill, nor are victims noted for the accuracy of their descriptions. The police could watch individuals with previous arrests or convictions for counterfeiting, but what of their right to privacy? Constitutional concerns arise with the prospect of making them routine subjects of surveillance.

The second question concerns what the police would be likely to see in the course of their visual surveillance. At the retail level, they might see the offender make a series of currency exchanges. But even if they observe a meeting between the retailer and a wholesaler, they are unlikely to see the counterfeit money itself be exchanged.

The use of a search warrant to seize contraband and other evidence is another commonly used investigative technique. To obtain one, the police must establish to judicial satisfaction the reliability of information that the contraband or other evidence is at the place to be searched. Where does this information come from? Usually from someone who has seen the evidence inside the place. Unless the informant is an undercover officer, the source of the information may be questionable, and the courts have fashioned a series of tests to screen out unreliable informants as part of the probable cause review mechanism.

The problems of outright perjury and planting of evidence are harder to deal with directly. The potential for gain provides real inducements for such conduct. The planting of evidence raises the possibility of the conviction of an individual on the basis of government-induced activity. A thorough search of an informant before a meeting with the subject of an investigation reduces the likelihood of misconduct, and careful instruction and supervision of informants can provide some safeguards against these abuses.[9]

Informants often are used to introduce an undercover agent to the subject of an investigation. This is an important and effective technique. The informant's introduction vouches for the legitimacy of the agent, but creates a danger for the informant once the agent's true identity emerges. But the law enforcement agency cannot control or even know what the informant says to the subject before introducing the agent, or at any time when the agent is not present. The inability to monitor the informant's behavior means that the informant may induce someone to participate in a criminal activity in which he or she would not otherwise be involved. It is here that the greatest danger of the agent provocateur emerges.

Many law enforcement agencies routinely record conversations between informants and subjects, both to monitor for inappropriate behavior and to provide evidence that such behavior did not occur. While this technique does not eliminate the possibility of misconduct by the informant, careful analysis of such conversations can offer hints of overreaching by the informant. Informants can be instructed to ask, in the course of recorded conversations, certain questions which may elicit information disclosing, or at least pointing to, such overreaching. Despite these safeguards, problems remain concerning the motivation, integrity, and reliability of informants because their behavior often is based on a desire for leniency, vengeance, or monetary gain.

Similar problems surround the testimony of co-conspirators, who often are motivated to portray the other parties to the crime in an unfavorable light in order to shift legal and moral responsibility to them. Law enforcement officials then are faced with a thicket of ethical issues in judging the relative culpability of the various parties in deciding what the charges should be. This problem can become particularly difficult when a case breaks open and there is a rush to the prosecutor's office by all or most of the offenders. The question then is who is the "little fish" whose testimony should be obtained by the promise of leniency in order successfully to prosecute the "bigger fish."

Law enforcement officials cannot avoid these problems because of the difficulty of discovering, much less successfully prosecuting, a clever conspiracy without the testimony of at least one of the parties. The use of co-conspirator testimony, like that of informant testimony, entails risks of perjury motivated by desire for vengeance or self-preservation. But without the use of these tainted tools, society must rely solely on infrequent fortuitous circumstances to protect important interests and values. Even the alternative techniques—such as electronic eavesdropping—usually require informant or co-conspirator cooperation or testimony in order to meet the probable cause standards for judicial authorization.

This array of difficulties is one of the primary reasons for the increased use of undercover agents.[10] Such agents are believed to be more reliable in and accountable for their actions. The desire for long-term career continuity can be a substantial inhibitor to misconduct for short-term gain in particular cases. Background screening and training are intended to provide agents of good character who have a clear understanding of the limits of permissible enforcement.

Careerism, of course, is a two-edged sword in this context. The desire to make a name for oneself can spur unscrupulous conduct. Further, the internal organizational pressures for productivity, necessary on one hand to ensure that the agents are diligent, tend to encourage overreaching. Theoretically, such misconduct would occur in the context of supervisory and administrative control structures which, at least at a level or two removed, would have much more to lose than to gain by

142

tolerating it. These administrative controls, combined with prosecutorial and judicial review, can limit the potential for abuse, although there is no question that they have sometimes failed, usually because the supervisory mechanism is co-opted or incompetent.[11]

The widespread adoption of audio and video devices to record agent-subject interactions arose in part from a desire to enhance control through a review capacity. The immediacy of the review these devices allow strengthens both administrative control and evidentiary presentation for the prosecution. Combined with careful physical surveillance and on-scene supervision, these safeguards can substantially reduce the risk of inappropriate inducement or entrapment by agents.[12]

The potential for physical danger to informants or co-conspirators who are induced to cooperate by the threat of legal sanctions poses another ethical problem. The government agent, who has accepted those risks as part of his or her employment or who faces only economic sanctions in refusing to undertake the role, is arguably a more appropriate person to bear those risks.

All of these techniques are more likely to result in successful investigations when clearly identifiable physical evidence is part of the criminal transaction. When it is not, for example the passing of unmarked or unrecorded currency in a bribery case, visual surveillance and authorized searches are less effective than they would be otherwise. Evidence of conversations about the conspiracy becomes crucial in establishing the requisite elements of the crime. That evidence can come only from human and electronic sources.[13] Further, electronic sources by themselves tend to cast such a wide net that their use in an investigation of a political figure is highly troubling. The potential for misuse of captured information irrelevant to legitimate investigative needs is so high as to justify only very limited use of electronic devices.

Testimony of agents or informants without electronic verification increases the vulnerability of the investigation to the motivational problems discussed above, as well as to misunderstanding or misinterpretation. Electronic verification both limits the invasion of privacy and inhibits impropriety by providing a review mechanism. Further, it confirms the details of the conversation.[14]

These safeguards do not eliminate all the difficulties and risks, one of the most troublesome being the behavior of agents (particularly informants or co-conspirators) before and outside of the recorded conversations. Nevertheless, a carefully planned investigation can expand the electronic coverage to record all significant conversation or to point, by means of intrinsic evidence, to conversations that may have been omitted.

In the context of this discussion of safeguards, a broader point needs to be made. In considering the costs and benefits of various investigative techniques, it is important to distinguish between errors in using a technique and inherent flaws in the tactic. The former can be corrected; the latter, if serious enough, may simply preclude use of the technique. The question to be posed is under what circumstances and with what limitations is this particular technique acceptable.

Use of Coercion and Deception in Investigations

This issue has been posed most sharply by the recently disclosed elaborate scenarios staged by the FBI in the course of its investigation of political corruption and other conspiratorial crimes. With the exception of apprehending an offender in the act in a retail-level counterfeiting transaction or similar situation, all of the investigative techniques are likely to involve some level of duplicity or deception either before or after the fact. In visual surveillance the techniques and disguises are designed to fool subjects into believing that they are unobserved. Informants, either on their own or as instructed by a government agent, are often betraying somebody's confidence. Co-conspirators who break faith with their partners are clearly being duplicitous. It is possible to draw a distinction between passive and active deception; between situations where the government takes advantage of the duplicity of others and those in which it creates the deception. Another distinction could be drawn between the government's allowing the subject to assume certain facts by creating certain circumstances and its making explicit statements that deceive the subject into committing a crime in the presence of government agents. The issue is whether these distinctions make a difference.

144

Testimony about the criminal transaction is essential to successful prosecution of most complainantless crimes. The use of coercion and of deception appear to be related inversely in many instances. The more heavily the government relies on informant or co-conspirator cooperation to build its cases, the more it has to invoke its coercive relationship with that person. On the other hand, government use of deception tends to be less blatant in these situations. When the government opts to investigate by means of its own undercover agent, it can reduce its demands on the coercive relationship with an informant or co-conspirator. The existence of this relationship between deception and coercion sharpens the ethical dilemma in formulating policy.

To strike the necessary balance in this matter it is appropriate to look more broadly at the use of deception in our society and the ethical and moral implications of its use. One need not be an overly cynical observer of the political process to conclude that the exercise of all political authority depends to some extent on the exercise of both deception and coercion, with the balance—in a democratic society—being struck in favor of deception. Ultimately the consequences of using deception must be balanced against the consequence of not using it. The administrative perspective suggests that fruitful consideration of these issues can occur only in the context of an understanding of the social values being protected, and of the realistic alternatives available to society for these purposes.

Gary T. Marx, in this thought-provoking analysis of some of these problems, has suggested an observation by sociologist Edward Shils as a starting point for such an endeavor: "Civil politics requires an understanding of the complexity of virtue, that no virtue stands alone, that every virtuous act costs something in terms of other virtuous acts, that virtues are intertwined with evil.[15]

This observation is true of both the exercise and the restraint of governmental authority.

NOTES

1. Gary T. Marx, "The New Police Undercover Work," *Urban Life* 8, *4* (January 1980); 399–446.

145

2. The argument asserts that by concentrating on "street" crime, law enforcement agencies are in fact pursuing a policy of differential enforcement aimed at the poor while at the same time ignoring the more lucrative crimes of the middle and upper classes.

3. See Marx, "The New Police Undercover Work."

4. "Power" is used to indicate clearly that we are talking about a capacity to impose or restrain the activity of others including agents of the government.

5. Misner and Clough provide an excellent example of this tendency when they dismiss the use of informants by law enforcement agents as a mere "convenience" but never seriously consider what resources are available to replace them. See Robert L. Misner and John H. Clough, "Arrestees as Informants: A Thirteenth Amendment Analysis," 29, *Stanford Law Review,* April 1977, pp. 713–46.

6. Statement of Thomas P. Sullivan, United States Attorney for the Northern District of Illinois, April 30, 1981.

7. Misner and Clough, "Arrestees as Informants."

8. Surveillance has become more sophisticated with the introduction of "bumper beepers," an electronic device which attaches to a car and sends out electronic signals. This device enhances the capacity of police to follow a vehicle without disclosing their presence. Most law enforcement agencies require supervisory approval before these devices can be used, and judicial approval if installation involves a trespass. Such devices can reduce the very substantial costs involved in maintaining an effective surveillance, particularly a moving surveillance.

9. These requirements include specifying the basis for believing that the informant is reliable; specifying the basis of the informants; corroboration for untested informants; timeliness of information.

10. The Drug Enforcement Agency (DEA), which relies heavily on informants in its investigations, has promulgated guidelines which attempt to assert administrative control over these individuals. The thrust of these regulations is to impose restrictions on who may be an informant and in what circumstances they may be used. The guidelines also require consultation with the appropriate U.S. attorney and the relevant law enforcement agency if a DEA agent has reason to believe that an informant has committed a serious criminal offense.

11. The U.S. Attorney General recently has issued extensive guidelines covering FBI undercover operations. The thrust of these guidelines is to ensure high level consideration of any sensitive undercover investigations and appropriate consultation with the relevant U.S. attorney or Strike Force attorneys when informants or agents are involved in an incident that is otherwise a serious crime. The guidelines do address the legal and ethical issues entailed in the creation of opportunities for illegal activities.

12. An old tactic, enjoying a revival, is the selling of a contraband substance to a subject by an undercover agent and then arresting the subject for possession of the contraband. This tactic seems to magnify the potential for entrapment and seems to me to be fundamentally unfair. My objection stems from a comparison of these situations with those in which the agent purchases the substance from the subject. In the latter instances the subject has the contraband in his possession (a violation in itself) thus giving evidence of willingness and ability to commit the illegal act. When large amounts of money and contraband are involved in the former cases, some, but not all, of the malaise is reduced. At the very least, these cases require close supervisory scrutiny.

146

13. Use of electronic devices requires a person who can testify to the requisite facts constituting probable cause. Thus, the same difficulties with inducements for informants and co-conspirators arise.
14. On the other hand, the possible use of electronic devices in an undercover investigation of a high-level organized crime figure is extremely difficult because of the precautions that they take as a matter of routine.
15. Gary T. Marx, "Who Really Gets Stung? Further Thoughts on Recent Police Undercover Activities." Gary T. Marx, "The Cost of Virtue," *The New York Times,* June 29, 1980.

About the Authors

GERALD M. CAPLAN, a professor at the George Washington University Law Center since 1977, was director of the National Institute of Justice in the U.S. Department of Justice from 1973 to 1977. Caplan, who has written widely on criminal justice issues, graduated from Northwestern University Law School and served as a prosecutor and general counsel to the Metropolitan Police in the District of Columbia.

WAYNE A. KERSTETTER, associate professor in the department of criminal justice at the University of Illinois at Chicago Circle, is also an affiliated scholar of the American Bar Foundation. His previous positions include superintendent of the Illinois Bureau of Investigation (1972–1976) and assistant first deputy police commissioner, New York City Police Department (1972–1973). He is a graduate of the University of Chicago Law School.

SANFORD V. LEVINSON, a professor at the University of Texas

148

Law School, is the editor of books on constitutional decisionmaking. He has a doctorate from Harvard University and is a graduate of Stanford University Law School.

GARY T. MARX, professor of sociology in the departments of urban studies and humanities at the Massachusetts Institute of Technology, is the author of *Protest and Prejudice* and editor of *Racial Conflict, Muckraking Sociology,* and other books. He is currently engaged in research on the social, ethical, and policy implications of undercover police work. Marx received his doctorate from the University of California at Berkeley.

MARK H. MOORE is a professor of criminal justice policy and management at Harvard University's Kennedy School of Government. He is the author of *Buy and Bust: The Effective Regulation of an Illicit Market in Heroin.* Moore has a doctorate in public policy from the Kennedy School.

IRVIN B. NATHAN coordinated the ABSCAM prosecutions when he served from 1979 to 1981 as deputy assistant attorney general in the U.S. Department of Justice. Now a partner in the Washington, D.C., law firm of Arnold and Porter, he is chairman of the White Collar Crime Committee of the American Bar Association and in 1981 served as special minority counsel to the Senate Intelligence Committee in its investigation of CIA Director William Casey. He is a graduate of Columbia University Law School.

PETER REUTER, senior economist at the Rand Corporation in Washington, D.C., is the author of the forthcoming *Illegal Markets: The Economics of the Visible Hand.* Reuter has done extensive research on the organization of illegal activities and, from 1974 to 1976, was research director for the Commission on the Review of the National Policy toward Gambling. He has a doctorate in economics from Yale.

LAWRENCE W. SHERMAN is director of research for the Police Foundation and associate professor of criminology at the University of Maryland. Sherman, who served as executive director of the National Advisory Commission on Higher Education for Police Officers, is the author and editor of several books, including *Ethics in Criminal Justice Education, Scandal and Reform: Controlling Police Corruption, The Police and Violence,* and *Police Corruption.* He has a doctorate in sociology from Yale University.

149

Index

Capone, Al, 74
Criden, Howard, 6-8
Civil liberties, 39, 67; and law
  enforcement, 18, 19, 23-28
Civiletti, Benjamin R., 14
Co-conspirators, 144-45; danger to,
  143; as witnesses, 22, 29, 142
Coercion, 68, 70-73, 76-77, 89, 94,
  144
COINTEL, 93
COINTELPRO, 103
Con games, 44, 45
Congress, 118, 126
Conspiracy, 76
Counterintelligence, 92
Courts, 39; U.S. Court of Appeals,
  2, 12
Crime: anticipated, 68, 90, 94;
  caused by undercover operations,
  89; classification of offenses,
  21-23; complaintantless. *See:
  Crime, complaintantless.*
  consensual, 67, 87; control,
  58-59; detected by decoys, 54;
  detected by informants, 33-35;
  detected by patrolling, 19, 29-37;
  detected by private individuals,
  19-20, 30, 32-33; detected by
  undercover operations, 35-36,
  54-55, 135-36; effect of undercover operations on, 86-90;
  extortionate, 22, 31; instigation
  of by government, 27-28, 35-36,
  107-9; invisible offenses. *See
  separate listing.* organized, 66,
  67, 69, 111; political, 31, 55, 89;
  reporting requirements, 32, 95;
  sampling theory of, 122-25;
  statistics, 124; street offenses,
  28-30, 37, 66; victimless, 21, 31,
  38, 120-21; white collar, 4, 21,

31, 66, 67, 111, 124. *See also
specific offenses: Bribery, Con
games, Vice, etc.*
Crime, complaintantless: characteristics of, 136-39; evidence of,
  139-40; jurisdiction in, 138-39;
  surveillance for, 140; testimony
  in, 145
Criminal Division (Justice Department), 5
Criminal justice reform, 67-69

Data processing techniques, 95
Deception/deceit, 29-30, 44-45,
  132; by government, 26-28,
  144-45; in investigations, 119-22,
  127-28, 129-30, 131, 144-45;
  by police, 53-54, 68, 94, 118-21;
  in undercover operations, 61
Decoy, 54, 88; anticrime, 66, 68,
  87; squads, 90; transactions, 10;
  in undercover operations, 85-87
Delany, Joe, 51-53, 55
DeVito, Tony (AKA Amoroso,
  Anthony), 7
Disguises, use of, 51, 53-54
Dix, George, 57
Drug Enforcement Administration
  (DEA), 102, 103, 109, 114

Elshtain, Jean Bethke, 46
Entrapment, 3, 68, 70, 73, 81, 143;
  in ABSCAM, 11-13; defined, 55;
  guidelines for prevention of,
  15-16
Equal Employment Opportunities
  Commission, 124
Errichetti, Angelo, 6-8, 9
Evidence, 139-40; gathering, 120-21;
  physical, 139, 143; planting, 141;
  videotapes as, 2, 5, 8, 13, 68,
  69, 143

Required reporting of crime, 32, 95
Right of privacy, 18, 23, 24, 29,
    37, 45-47, 53, 59, 76, 90, 121;
    invasion of, 143; and undercover
    operations, 51
Right of silence, 59-60, 61
Robinson, Donald, 73

Sampling theory (of crime), 122-25
Search warrants, 16, 141
Searches, 143; probable cause
    requirement for, 24; and seizures,
    68
Self-incrimination, 59-60
Sherman v. United States, 75
Shils, Edward, 145
Silvestri, Joseph, 81
Stewart, Potter, 54
Stimpson, Henry, 90
Sting operations, 13-14, 15, 87-88;
    federal, 14
Sting, The, 43-44
Stowe, John, 8
Street Crime Unit, 87
Social control (of crime), 90-96
Special Investigations Unit (NYPD),
    106
Sullivan, Thomas, 138
Sullivan, William, 92
Supreme Court, 3, 54-55, 56, 67
Surveillance, 90, 120; covert, 20, 21,
    26, 29-30; electronic, 53-55, 76,
    142, 143; by government, 23-26,
    29, 33, 38; for invisible offenses,
    30-32; overt, 28-29; private, 33;
    routine physical, 31; targets for,
    25, 29; technology, 69; visual,
    140, 143, 144. *See also:
    Information gathering tech-
    niques.*

Tape recordings, 16, 53, 81, 141,
    143, 144

"Target weakening," 91
Targets: for ABSCAM, 4, 85; and
    administrative rolemaking,
    128-30; for criminal investiga-
    tion, 119, 125-28; group, 127-28;
    individual, 131-33; for informa-
    tion gathering techniques, 25;
    for narcotics investigation, 108-9;
    selection of, 122-23, 125, 127,
    129-32; for surveillance, 25, 29;
    for undercover operations, 70-72,
    75-77, 80-81, 89
Teapot Dome, 3
Temptation, 70-72, 73-75, 89
Testimonial privileges, 56
Thirteenth Amendment, 140
Thompson, Frank, Jr., 8, 72
Toxic waste disposal (illegal), 22
Trammel v. United States, 56
Trickery, 70-72

Undercover operations, 1, 18, 65, 66,
    68, 76, 90, 121; advantages of,
    69; use of brokers in, 81; changes
    in, 67; use of coercion in, 72-73;
    in consensual crimes, 67; crime
    caused by, 89; crime detected by,
    35-36, 54-55, 135-36; and
    damage to third parties, 83-86;
    deception in, 61; use of decoys
    in, 85-87; disadvantages of,
    69-70; in drug offenses, 66, 69;
    effect on crime, 86-90; and
    entrapment, 70; federal, 3-4, 67,
    82-84, 93; federal guidelines for,
    14-16; financing of, 69, 78, 93;
    future use of, 4; and infiltration,
    52-59; and informants, 48, 66,
    80-83; and instigation, 35-36;
    for invisible offenses, 21; and law
    enforcement strategy, 20; use of
    middlemen in, 81; objections to,
    55; and police, 69, 91-96;

155